HEALTHY
WOOD PELLET
Grill & Smoker
— COOKBOOK —

HEALTHY
WOOD PELLET
Grill & Smoker
— COOKBOOK —

Nancy Loseke
with foreword by Steven Raichlen

ALPHA

Publisher Mike Sanders
Editor Christopher Stolle
Art Director William Thomas
Compositor Ayanna Lacey
Photographer Daniel Showalter
Food Stylist Lovoni Walker
Proofreaders Diane Durrett & Christopher Parris
Indexer Louisa Emmons

First American Edition, 2020
Published in the United States by DK Publishing
6081 E. 82nd Street, Indianapolis, Indiana 46250

20 21 22 23 24   10 9 8 7 6 5 4 3 2 1
001-317264-MAY2020

ISBN: 978-1-4654-9262-3
Library of Congress Catalog Number: 2019950802

Note: This publication contains the opinions and ideas of its
authors. It is intended to provide helpful and informative material
on the subject matter covered. It is sold with the understanding
that the author(s) and publisher are not engaged in rendering
professional services in the book. If the reader requires personal
assistance or advice, a competent professional should be
consulted. The authors and publisher specifically disclaim any
responsibility for any liability, loss, or risk, personal or otherwise,
which is incurred as a consequence, directly or indirectly, of the
use and application of any of the contents of this book.

Trademarks: All terms mentioned in this book that are known to
be or are suspected of being trademarks or service marks have
been appropriately capitalized. Alpha Books, DK, and Penguin
Random House LLC cannot attest to the accuracy of this
information. Use of a term in this book should not be regarded as
affecting the validity of any trademark or service mark.
DK books are available at special discounts when purchased in
bulk for sales promotions, premiums, fund-raising, or educational
use. For details, contact SpecialSales@dk.com.

Printed and bound in China

A WORLD OF IDEAS:
SEE ALL THERE IS TO KNOW

www.dk.com

Contents

Salt & Pepper Dinosaur Bones (p. 46)

Pig on a Stick (p. 88)

Oysters Margarita (p. 131)

Korean Pulled Pork Lettuce Wraps (p. 77)

Grilled Peaches with Raspberry Sauce (p. 169)

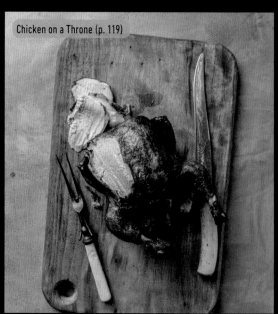

Chicken on a Throne (p. 119)

Foreword by Steven Raichlen

I never met a grill book I didn't love.

But this one holds special significance because it was written by my longtime friend and assistant, Nancy Loseke.

Yes, *that* Nancy—the content director of my barbecuebible.com website, the editor of my *Up in Smoke* newsletter, the culinary producer of my shows on American Public Television, the Nancy who painstakingly proofreads all my books, tests the recipes, and lends such a big helping hand at Barbecue University, the barbecue boot camp I founded 20 years ago.

And now to her long list of accomplishments in the barbecue world, add Nancy's first book.

It's about a subject that is hot, hot, hot in the barbecue world—and I don't just mean on account of fire. Her *Healthy Wood Pellet Grill & Smoker Cookbook* addresses two of the biggest trends in American barbecue: healthy grilling and pellet grills. Because, let's face it, much as we all love that plate-burying rack of ribs or brisket, too much barbecued meat might wind up burying us. More and more of us—and that certainly includes me—are trying to incorporate grilled seafood, vegetables, grains, and other healthy ingredients into our diets. Nancy is ready to oblige us with the delectable likes of lean and

low-carb Chuckwagon Beef Jerky, Thai-Style Swordfish Steaks with Peanut Sauce, and Roasted Parmesan-Crusted Whole Cauliflower. That's not to say Nancy shies away from meat: Her Buffalo-Glazed Bison Burgers, Tuscan Cheesesteaks, and Pig on a Stick will make the heart of any diehard carnivore beat faster.

The other trend Nancy addresses is pellet grills. You don't need a degree in marketing to know that this is the fastest-growing segment of the grill market. New brands are proliferating (Weber just got into the act) and existing brands become more sophisticated every day. You can now control your Green Mountain Pellet Grill, for example, with your smartphone. Having worked for many years for pellet grill pioneer Traeger, Nancy has more than a decade of experience with pellet grills. She'll teach you how to get maximum performance out of your grill.

The *Healthy Wood Pellet Grill & Smoker Cookbook* by Nancy Loseke. I'm proud to add this book to my library and I know you'll be glad you've added it to yours.

Steven Raichlen

Miami, Florida
November 2019

Introduction

Wood pellet grills are arguably the biggest development in the grilling industry since the 1950s, when Chicago welder George Stephen fabricated a lidded grill—later known as a kettle grill—from a marine buoy and the first gas grill, called a Lazy-Man, was introduced to the world.

With Wi-Fi connectivity, digital controllers, sleeker designs, and higher temperature differentials with searing capability, pellet grills have an allure not seen in other grills. They offer the primal thrill of grilling with wood smoke coupled with the turn-of-the-knob convenience normally associated with kitchen appliances. No longer is it necessary to find a sustainable source of wood, chop it, season it, or store it. Or labor to build and maintain a steady fire and the blue smoke prized by old-school pitmasters. Until recently, pellet grills were disparaged—even banned—on the competition barbecue circuit, with the implication being they were "too easy." But people weren't buying the premise that barbecue had to be "hard" to be authentic. What they were buying was pellet grills. Millions of them are now in backyards, perfuming entire neighborhoods with fragrant wood smoke.

Although I had previous experience with kettle grills, hybrid fuel grills, kamado-style cookers, offset barrel smokers, hibachis, gas grills, and even a Brazilian rodizio, I was unfamiliar with pellet grills until 2009, when the CEO of a major player in the pellet grill field phoned with a proposition: Write a cookbook that would give new pellet grill owners a blueprint for success and he would send me an array of pellet grills and a regular paycheck. My first pellet grill arrived days later and it was love at first bite. Grilling was fun again! And it continues to be. (Today, that spiral-bound cookbook still accompanies the company's pellet grills.)

An unanticipated benefit of my introduction to wood pellet grilling was that despite cooking more, I regained control of my weight and carb intake. Lean proteins, like pork tenderloin and chicken breasts, which often dry out on conventional grills, were juicy and succulent. Wood-charred broccoli needed just a drizzle of olive oil and salt and pepper to make it delicious. Grilled stone fruits with an ounce or two of cheese made for a splendid dessert. Pellet grilling and smoking thus became a way of life. Whether you're a seasoned veteran or new to pellet grilling, I hope the information and recipes in these pages inspire your grilling and smoking and help you achieve your health goals. Keep the smoke rolling!

Nancy Loseke

Moreland Hills, Ohio
November 2019

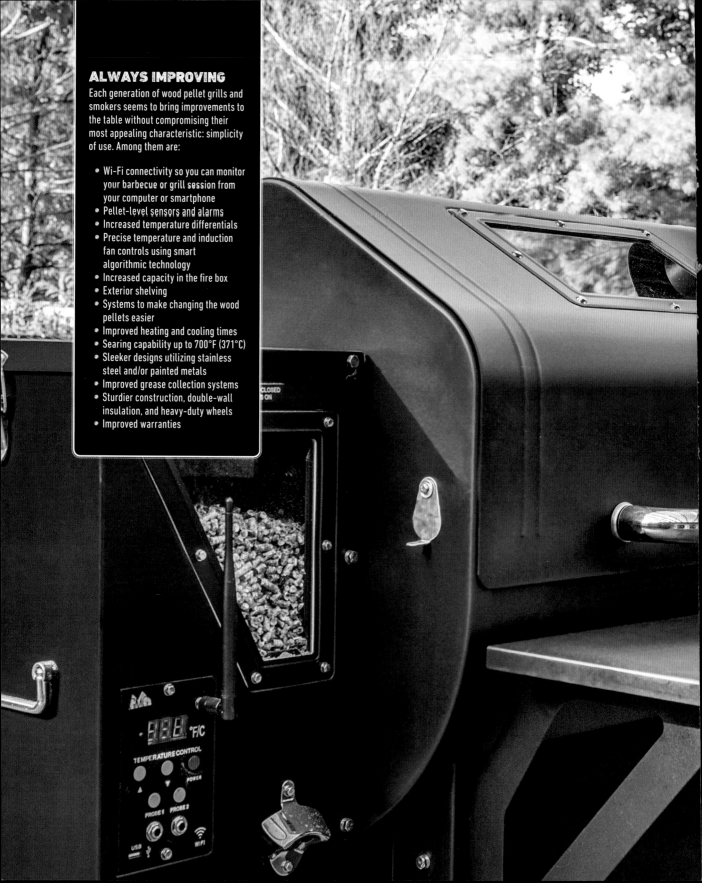

ALWAYS IMPROVING

Each generation of wood pellet grills and smokers seems to bring improvements to the table without compromising their most appealing characteristic: simplicity of use. Among them are:

- Wi-Fi connectivity so you can monitor your barbecue or grill session from your computer or smartphone
- Pellet-level sensors and alarms
- Increased temperature differentials
- Precise temperature and induction fan controls using smart algorithmic technology
- Increased capacity in the fire box
- Exterior shelving
- Systems to make changing the wood pellets easier
- Improved heating and cooling times
- Searing capability up to 700°F (371°C)
- Sleeker designs utilizing stainless steel and/or painted metals
- Improved grease collection systems
- Sturdier construction, double-wall insulation, and heavy-duty wheels
- Improved warranties

Wood Pellet Grills
A Brief History

Some historians trace the genesis of the wood pellet grill to the oil crisis of 1973 and the subsequent emergence in the Pacific Northwest of compressed wood pellets as an alternative to home heating oil.

Maybe. But the story Traeger features on its website sounds more plausible: Joe Traeger, a principal in Traeger Heating of Mt. Angel, Oregon, stepped away from the 1985 Fourth of July festivities to check on the family's barbecued chicken and found it—and his gas grill—in flames. His experience with stoves for home heating meant he was well positioned to develop a pellet-fueled grill and smoker that he could trust with a whole chicken.

Patterned after the serious-looking offset smokers popular in Texas and Oklahoma oil country, his invention was patented in 1986. For two decades, industry pioneer Traeger had the market for pellet grills and smokers mostly to itself. Then its patent expired. Within the year, Traeger had formidable competition from such companies as Louisiana Grills, Green Mountain Grills, MAK, and others.

Today, there are more than 35 manufacturers of wood pellet grills, including iconic grill companies Weber and Kingsford. Many have gotten into the business in the last five years.

Cooking with wood pellets might seem like a fad, but with more and more people using wood pellet grills, the evidence seems clear: This combination grill and smoker is here to stay. It'll change the way we eat and introduce future generations to the pleasures of cooking with wood smoke.

And remember Joe Traeger's ruined chicken? Today, salespeople for the company invite potential customers to take the "Chicken Challenge," which calls for roasting a 4-pound (1.8kg) chicken at 375°F (191°C) for 70 minutes. If you accept this challenge, you'll be rewarded with having cooked the most delicious bird you've ever put on your wood pellet grill and smoker.

How a Wood Pellet Grill & Smoker Works

These electric outdoor devices might look intimidating. However, their versatility allows you to barbecue, grill, smoke, roast, braise, and, yes, even bake. But are they a grill or a smoker?

Actually, they're both, although they perform more like a convection oven. With the press of an ignition button or the turn of a knob, you can unleash the food-enhancing power of wood smoke. Aside from their digital and algorithmic trappings, they're simple devices.

Small cylindrical pellets made of compressed hardwood sawdust in the hopper start and fuel the fire. (Only the wood's natural lignin holds the pellets together, so it's important to keep them dry.) At a rate controlled by the set temperature, the pellets drop through the bottom of the hopper and are carried to the fire box (sometimes called the fire pot) in the belly of the cook chamber by a screw-like auger. There, a small heat rod is activated for a few minutes, igniting the pellets.

A removable baffle—like a roof over the fire box—diffuses the heat while an induction fan located near the hopper circulates the hot air and smoke evenly throughout the cook chamber. The rate of pellet delivery is managed by a built-in sensor and plays a critical role in maintaining the set temperature. Just like a campfire, the more wood added, the hotter the fire. Fat and juices from food on the grill grate fall onto an angled grease pan and are channeled to a removable collection container, usually on the grill's exterior. This makes cleanup easier.

When you close the grill lid, you're infusing what you're cooking with wood smoke while also giving the food a grilled patina that enriches and enhances the flavor inside—a great way for an amateur chef to feel like a seasoned pitmaster.

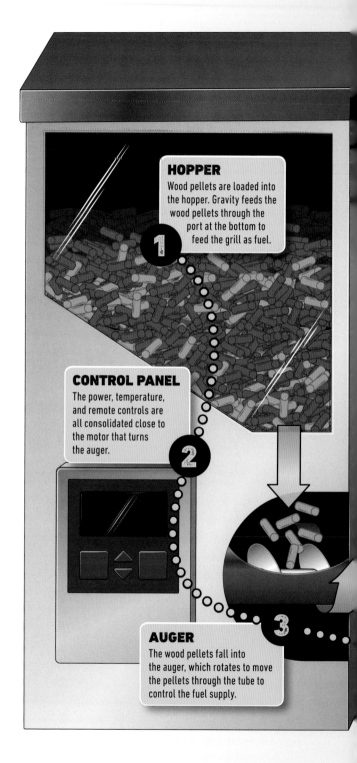

HOPPER
Wood pellets are loaded into the hopper. Gravity feeds the wood pellets through the port at the bottom to feed the grill as fuel.

CONTROL PANEL
The power, temperature, and remote controls are all consolidated close to the motor that turns the auger.

AUGER
The wood pellets fall into the auger, which rotates to move the pellets through the tube to control the fuel supply.

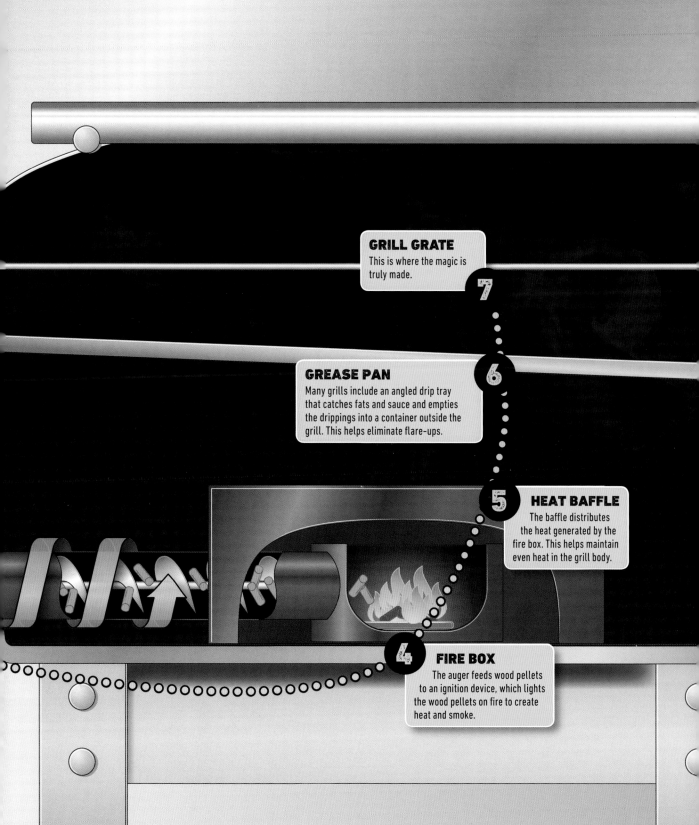

GRILL GRATE
This is where the magic is truly made.

7

6

GREASE PAN
Many grills include an angled drip tray that catches fats and sauce and empties the drippings into a container outside the grill. This helps eliminate flare-ups.

5

HEAT BAFFLE
The baffle distributes the heat generated by the fire box. This helps maintain even heat in the grill body.

4

FIRE BOX
The auger feeds wood pellets to an ignition device, which lights the wood pellets on fire to create heat and smoke.

Which Pellets to Choose?
A Quick Primer

When wood pellet grill enthusiasts get together—in person or via social media channels—there's a lot of discussion about which wood pellets to use when smoking, barbecuing, or grilling their favorite foods.

Some have very precise formulas they follow, particularly if they're competition-level barbecuers. Even pellet manufacturers have jumped in with both feet, creating blends they believe are optimum for pork, beef, poultry, seafood, and other foods. Some peddle pellets infused with wine, beer, or whiskey or that are formulated especially for game meats.

With all the combinations out there, it's difficult to make specific recommendations. But it's good to remember that the unique flavors of regional American barbecue were shaped by what woods were historically available. In the Pacific Northwest, alder was the choice for fresh seafood, especially salmon; oak and mesquite fueled the beef-centric barbecue in Texas, and although strong flavored, both are still great woods for brisket or steak; the Southeast up into the Carolinas relied on their native hickory, pecan, and peach trees, especially for pork, poultry, and Brunswick stew; maple wood was the choice of New Englanders to flavor such specialties as turkey, chicken, pork, and baked beans.

Most of the aforementioned woods are available in pellet form, as are apple and cherry, which are good picks when a fruity, mild flavor is required. If you're new to pellet grilling, worry less about flavors and more about finding a reliable supplier—a source for pellets that burn cleanly and predictably at a reasonable cost. (There will be time to experiment later.) Buy pellets that are actually made from the hardwoods advertised on the front of the bag—real hickory, mesquite, cherry wood, etc. Some brands are made with cheap hardwoods and then infused with flavored oils—and you don't want those.

TYPES OF WOOD PELLETS

While the type of wood you use does affect flavors some, it's more important to choose quality wood pellets made from reliable sources. The best wood is what you have on hand.

LIGHTER SMOKE AND FLAVOR

APPLE

A slightly sweet smoke that works beautifully with pork and poultry.

CHERRY

Flavorful and hearty smoke great for about anything.

PECAN

A favorite in the Carolinas, where this nutty wood is native.

ALDER

Favored in the Pacific Northwest and offers plenty of smoke without overwhelming delicate flavors.

MAPLE

Mild, with a hint of sweetness. A favorite in New England for pork and vegetables.

OAK

Stronger than fruitwoods but not as strong as hickory or mesquite. Great for brisket or steak.

MESQUITE

Almost synonymous with Texas barbecue. Provides a very robust smoke flavor.

HICKORY

Extremely popular in barbecue. Has a strong flavor that complements most meats.

BOLDER SMOKE AND FLAVOR

Maintaining Your Pellet Grill & Smoker

Because you want your wood pellet grill and smoker to last for many years, you should take measures to protect it. This includes having a cover for it as well as storing it away from the elements between uses, especially given the electronics involved. But you should also follow these recommendations to ensure you can always get the most from your wood pellet grill and smoker.

After each use

If possible, immediately after taking the food off the grill and before the grill cools down, spritz the grate lightly with water and use a grill brush or scraper to remove any bits of food. (It's like deglazing a pan with water or another liquid—the brown bits loosen immediately.) Remove the grease bucket if your grill has one and dispose of the contents. Store the bucket where pets or other animals can't get to it. Some pellet grillers tuck foil liners in their buckets, but this isn't necessary. Let the grill cool completely and then use a natural spray cleanser and paper towels to remove any grease smudges, sauce drips, etc. Use a special stainless steel cleaner and/or polish if your grill has stainless parts.

Before and during startup

Lift the grill lid and check to make sure there's nothing in the grill, like a stray pair of tongs, a forgotten chicken wing, etc. If necessary, change the aluminum foil on your drip pan. Clean and replace the grease bucket if needed. Start your grill according to the manufacturer's instructions and set it for your desired temperature. When the grill grate has reached the set temperature, brush it once more with a grill brush or scraper. (Use brass bristles for porcelain- or enamel-coated grill grates.) Stainless steel grates can be returned to nearly new condition by using a pumice stone on them, often found where grill supplies are sold. Be sure to wipe the grate down well with a damp paper towel to remove any grit. Oil the grill grate by dipping a folded paper towel in vegetable oil, clasping it in tongs, and running it along the bars of the grate. This will especially keep food from sticking to the grill grate, but it's also a great way to not have extra cleanup after grilling.

Periodically

Depending on how often you use your pellet grill and smoker, you'll want to vacuum the cook chamber and pellet hopper with a shop vacuum to remove any accumulation of ash and/or sawdust or loose pellets. (If possible, dedicate a small vacuum to this use only.) Other helpful cleaning tools are a putty knife for baked-on debris and smoke residue; a small shovel; and a metal spoon or small measuring cup for cleaning out the fire pot.

Be sure the holes around the periphery of the pot are clear. Carefully wipe down the temperature sensor. (Check your owner's manual for its location.) Don't forget the chimney and chimney cap. For this, you can use a damp scrubby attached to the handle of a wooden spoon with thick rubber bands.

If your grill begins to exhibit signs of rust, treat the areas with high-temperature paint before the problem expands.

Equipment & Accessories

If you have a reasonably well-equipped kitchen, you can begin cooking on your pellet grill right after the initial burn-in. (See your owner's manual for instructions on how to do it.) But there are a few accessories and pieces of equipment that will make your grilling/smoking experiences more pleasurable. Here are some of the items you can add to your outdoor *batterie de cuisine*.

Grill Gloves/Insulated Food-Safe Gloves

Invest in a sturdy pair of long-sleeved grill gloves made of leather or silicone to protect your hands from hot surfaces. Welder's gloves or fireplace gloves are often more substantial than those sold with grilling equipment. Rubberized insulated food gloves are also a good investment, enabling you to pull hot pork shoulder or move hams, turkeys, or other large cuts of meat to a platter or cutting board.

Grill Brush

The Centers for Disease Control reports that consumers occasionally ingest wire bristles from cheaply made grill brushes. Buy bristle-free wooden scrapers or brushes with bristles that are woven into the head. If your grill grate is coated with porcelain, look for brushes with brass bristles to avoid damaging the grate. Otherwise, stainless steel brushes are acceptable.

Food Thermometer

There are many types of thermometers on the market—from digital instant-read thermometers to remote multiple probe thermometers that can monitor several foods at once. Look for a thermometer that gives you a quick and accurate reading with enough range to suit your habits and a slender probe for testing the temperature of thin fish fillets or similar foods. Some pellet grills have built-in remote thermometers. (Dome thermometers are useless and only measure the temperature at the peak of the grill lid. Don't rely on them.)

Heavy-Duty Foil and Disposable Pans

Most pellet grill manufacturers recommend covering the drip plate with aluminum foil for easier clean-up. Find 18-inch (46cm) rolls of heavy-duty foil at most grocery stores. While you're there, pick up a stack of aluminum foil roasting pans in various sizes, preferably with lids. They're especially handy when you tote food to another location, such as brisket, ribs, or pulled pork.

Long-Handled Barbecue Tools

Short tongs will be a hindrance when you're reaching over a hot grill grate to turn chicken wings. Shop for such tools as tongs, basting brushes, and spatulas with 18-inch (46cm) handles to avoid singeing your forearms—or worse.

Rib Rack

Ribs can take up a lot of real estate on a grill—problematic if you own one of the smaller pellet grills. Increase the number of racks your grill can accommodate by buying a rib rack, which supports a vertical orientation—sometimes up to six racks.

Grill Basket or Tray

Perforated grill baskets or trays prevent sacrifices to the grill gods by corralling such small foods as shrimp, mushrooms, asparagus spears, mussels, etc. If you love seafood, buy a hinged locking device made from wire mesh. You can then turn delicate fish fillets without fear of them falling apart.

Grill Mats

These pliant, nonstick mats, which resemble plastic-coated shelf liners, can be cut to size to fit your grill. They work well for fish, vegetables, and even meatloaf. They can't be exposed to direct flame, making them perfect for the diffused heat of pellet grills.

GrillGrates

One barbecue entrepreneur patented these interlocking panels that fit right on top of your grill grate. They channel heat to the raised aluminum rails, producing excellent grill marks. They're a little pricey, but worth it if you love grilled steaks, chops, chicken breasts, burgers, etc.

Cold Smoker

A cold smoker is essentially an add-on chamber that connects to the chimney side of your grill to keep the food being smoked from the heat source. The temperature generally exceeds what's used for cold smoking (80 to 100°F or 27 to 38° C). So you might save cold-smoking projects for cool days or nights. For a cheaper alternative, buy a smoker maze or tube.

Smoker Maze or Tube

For more flavor, you can augment the smoke generated by using a maze or tube, which burns pellets. (The latter can smoke for up to 12 hours.) You can also use it for cold-smoking such foods as cheese, fish, eggs, etc. For efficient lighting, use a small torch.

Cast Iron Skillets and Grill Pans

Two reasons why pellet grills don't produce good grill marks: 1) Porcelain or stainless steel grates don't transfer heat efficiently to the surface of the food and 2) the maximum temperature the grill reaches is often 450°F (232°C)—far less than temperatures used in steak houses. Preheat a ridged cast iron grill pan or skillet when you light the grill to help achieve good caramelization and amazing grill marks.

Pellet Bin

Wood pellets are hydroscopic, meaning they're quick to absorb water if exposed to humid environments. If they don't collapse completely, they'll fail to burn properly and can even jam the auger. Store them in a dry place in a sturdy lidded container. Some people use the pail certain brands of kitty litter come in.

Head Lamp

Unless your outdoor grilling area is exceptionally well lit, a bright head lamp will illuminate the dark interior of your grill before the sun rises or after the sun sets. Buy one that's not only rechargeable but also waterproof.

Meat Slicer

Although not a "must have," a meat slicer for home use is handy if you make your own bacon, smoked ham, pastrami, beef jerky, etc. It will give you professional-looking results.

Spice/Coffee Grinder

If you like to make your own barbecue rubs or ensure a supply of freshly ground pepper, a sturdy electric spice/coffee grinder is a big help.

Shop or Fireplace Vacuum

Because it burns wood, your pellet grill will accumulate fine ash in the bottom of the fire box and the fire pot itself. A shop-type or fireplace vac, preferably with a metal canister, is invaluable for removing ash.

Safety Tips

Because wood pellet grills have more in common with convection ovens than gas or charcoal grills, it's easy to forget there's live fire under that diffuser plate. Below are a few suggestions to keep you safe and your wood pellet grill functioning properly for years to come.

- Read the instruction manual that came with your grill (if the paper copy has been lost or misplaced, most brands link to specific models online) and follow the directions for proper setup and shutoff procedures.

- Position your wood pellet grill away from any structures, wooden railings, siding, soffits, overhanging tree branches, etc. Poor grill hygiene and/or improper startups and shutdowns can cause pellet smokers to flame-out, blowing the lid open and causing flames to shoot several feet in the air.

- Never use your grill in an enclosed area, such as a garage, porch, or other structure. Carbon monoxide can build up and is very deadly.

- Only use food-safe pellets in your grill. Inferior brands or pellets intended for use in stoves might contain varnish, glue, paint, and remnants (including metal filings) from other manufacturing processes.

- The design of many pellet hoppers (the receptacle that holds the pellets) is flawed in that pellets can build up in the corners of the hopper while starving the auger. When this happens, the set temperature will drop and you'll be forced to restart your grill according to the manufacturer's instructions. (You can't add more pellets to the empty hopper and hope for the best. This can cause a dramatic flameout.) It's important to periodically check on the pellet level during a cook. Try to keep the hopper half full or more at all times.

- If you see smoke leaking from the lid of the pellet hopper (this is called a back-burn), turn off the grill, unplug it, and let it cool completely. Call the manufacturer's customer service department and describe the problem before attempting to relight the grill.

- Don't plug rear vents or reduce the distance between the chimney and the chimney cap in an effort to retain more smoke in the fire box.

- Most manufacturers will advise you to clean your pellet grill after five cooks. But it's advisable to clean the grill after long cooks, especially those involving such fatty meats as whole pigs, ducks, etc. A buildup of ash and grease can cause your grill to catch on fire.

- Keep a fully charged multipurpose fire extinguisher and a bucket of sand or salt near your grill in case of emergency. (The sand or salt will help extinguish grease fires.) If you are unsure of the readiness of your fire extinguisher, your local fire department should be able to check it for you.

- Follow good food safety practices when grilling outdoors. To avoid food-borne illnesses, keep cold foods cold and hot foods hot. Avoid cross-contamination by washing any plates, platters, or utensils that have come in contact with raw food.

- Despite the oft-quoted pellet grill mantra "Set it and forget it," check your pellet grill often when in use and don't leave it unattended for long periods of time.

Cold Weather Grilling

There was a time when Americans living in four-season climates wintered their grills in their garages from Labor Day until Memorial Day. No more! With a few adjustments to your routine you can still enjoy foods prepared on your wood pellet grill even when temperatures dip.

Stock up on pellets: Depending on the weather conditions, you might notice a surge in wood pellet consumption when the snow flies or the wind blows. Most pellet grills use about ½ pound (225g) of pellets on the Smoke or lowest setting and 3 pounds (1.4kg) of pellets on the High setting. But the amount of pellets required to maintain your set temperature can increase by as much as 25% or more. Have an extra bag (or two) on hand to avoid running out.

Get out of the wind: If it's an option, move your grill out of the wind. However, don't be tempted to move it into the garage or an enclosed porch or a high traffic area.

Allow extra time: Weather can affect startup and cooking times. Allow an extra 10 minutes or more for your grill to reach its set temperature. (In cold weather, it's a good idea to heat your grill incrementally, as some of the internal parts of the grill can be sluggish.) To be on the safe side, also add as much as 25% to the expected length of your cooks.

Clear the grill and the area around it of snow and ice: True winter warriors will shovel a path to their grill before they tackle the driveway or sidewalk! Sprinkle sidewalk salt on any slippery patches to avoid accidents.

Dress for success: Dress for the appropriate conditions, but avoid extra puffy coats and dangling waist, hat, or hood cords. Also, protect your hands with heat-resistant grill gloves—not ski gloves.

Cover the grill: A grill cover is a good investment no matter what weather your grill will be exposed to. In colder climates, the insulated grill blankets or jackets some pellet grill manufacturers sell are worth the money. They do seem to retain the grill's heat, particularly when the grill is made from thinner metals.

Light the area: Because winter days are notoriously short, make sure the grill and your work station are well lit. A flashlight or headlamp will help illuminate the dark interior of the grill. If at all possible, try to start your cooks well before you know darkness will descend.

Select foods with shorter cooking times: For your own comfort and to save money on pellets, select foods that cook quickly—in an hour or less. Chicken breasts, fish fillets, shrimp, steaks, burgers, brats, chops, and pork tenderloin medallions are all good choices.

"If you're lookin', you're not cookin'": This popular saying in barbecue circles is especially true in inclement weather. Try to avoid opening the grill lid more than necessary because it will take your grill extra time to regenerate lost heat.

Keep the food hot: Transporting food even a short distance (from the grill to the kitchen) can cause food to cool quickly. Have a small insulated cooler (warmed first with hot water) at the ready or heat a cast iron skillet on the grill while you're cooking and transfer the food to it before starting the journey to the table.

Strategies for Adding Flavor

In addition to cooking over wood smoke, there are other techniques you can use to boost the appeal of your grilled and smoked food. For example, you can grill or smoke almost any cut of meat with just salt and pepper and they'll be delectable. But you can enliven those and other foods with rubs, sauces, brines, and other mixtures you can use before, during, and after cooking.

Rubs

Dry rubs are the easiest way to flavor grilled foods. They're mixtures that generally combine salt, spices and herbs, and sometimes sugar. They're sprinkled over food, usually shortly before the cook.

Commercial rubs are formulated for specific proteins, such as poultry, beef, pork, seafood, and game meats. Some specialty rubs emulate the flavors of specific cuisines, such as Caribbean (think spicy jerk seasoning), Mexican, Kansas City–style, etc. But the real fun comes when you begin making your own rubs. They can be as simple as coarse salt (kosher or sea), freshly ground black pepper, and crushed red pepper flakes, which is what many pitmasters use on brisket. Or they can be complex, with the addition of many spices and other ingredients. You can even add the umami flavors of dried Worcestershire powder or dried porcini to your rubs. Be sure to record your recipe using exact amounts so you can replicate your successes.

Sometimes called spice pastes, wet rubs are another option. Resembling a purée, they're made "wet" by the addition of water, oil, juice, yogurt, mayo, mustard, beer, etc. They can also contain fresh aromatics, such as fresh herbs, garlic, chili peppers, or onion They're spread on the food usually several hours before the cook session and they're similar to marinades in their seasoning power.

Marinades

Most marinades contain an oil (such as olive oil or vegetable oil), an acid (wine, vinegar, citrus juice, etc.), seasonings (salt and pepper at the least), and various aromatics and/or fresh herbs. Essentially, they're vinaigrettes. Other common ingredients include Dijon mustard, soy sauce, tamari, or Worcestershire sauce. While it was once thought that marinades tenderize meat, they don't penetrate deeply (only about ¼ inch [.5cm]). But they still add flavor to the surface. Soak the meat for 2 to 4 hours before you're ready to grill. A general ratio to follow is 3 parts oil to 1 part acid. If there's just a little bit of Dijon mustard left in a jar, you can add the juice of half a lemon, some olive oil, and salt and pepper to taste. Replace the lid, shake vigorously, and voilà!—a marinade that costs almost nothing. Marinades are best on kebabs, flank steak, chops, pork, chicken breasts, and even vegetables.

Bastes

At their most elemental, bastes are thin liquids that are applied during the cook (either with a spray bottle, a basting brush, or a barbecue mop) to keep the meat moist while cooking. Examples include fruit juice, beer, broth, brewed coffee, or soda. Other ingredients, such as butter or oil, are also sometimes added. On long cooks, start basting the meat after the first hour. Any sooner than that and you'll displace any seasonings you sprinkled on the meat.

Sauces

While this category includes the tomato-based, sweetish sauces commonly associated with American barbecue, there's a whole world out there! You can experience the unique regional sauces that evolved in the United States—among them, the piquant vinegar- and mustard-based sauces found in the Carolinas, Alabama's white barbecue sauce (page 24), and Baltimore's pungent horseradish sauce (page 25). But you can also enjoy Thailand's peanut sauce (page 25), citrusy ponzu from Japan, chimichurri from South America, and garlicky aioli. Most sauces are served on the side, but they can also be applied during the last few minutes of cooking so any sugars in them don't scorch.

Wet and Dry Brines

One of my favorite techniques for flavoring and tenderizing poultry, pork, and seafood is wet brining. I can't imagine making the Thanksgiving turkey without soaking it for 12 hours in a simple solution of kosher salt and water—1 cup of Morton's kosher salt (it measures differently than other brands) to 1 gallon (3.8 liters) of distilled water. Sometimes, I get fancy and add apple cider, bourbon, or maple syrup. In any case, the bird is always incredibly juicy. (You can even brine pork chops in dill pickle juice. Try it!)

Soaking food in salt and water to preserve it and make it more palatable is an ancient technique. In fact, sea water is thought to be the original brine. But when refrigeration replaced traditional curing and preserving methods, brining apparently fell out of favor with home cooks. In the early 2000s, a popular cooking magazine published a primer on brining and a new generation was in brining's thrall.

Unlike marinades, brines do cause changes deep in the meat. The salt unwinds the proteins (imagine a strand of yarn that's been untwisted), creating gaps that trap water, making the meat juicier and more flavorful. A test conducted by the aforementioned magazine concluded that brined turkeys weighed 6 to 8 ounces more (170 to 225g) after roasting than unbrined birds.

Dry brining affects the proteins similarly and many food writers now recommend it over wet brining. (For sure, it takes up less space in the refrigerator because it doesn't require gallons of water or a real estate–grabbing container.) You season the protein with salt or a salt-based rub (about 1 tablespoon per 5 pounds [2.3kg]) of meat is the favored formula) and refrigerate it for a time determined by its size and thickness. (A turkey could take 2 days, while shrimp or delicate fish fillets need only 15 minutes.) The salt is rinsed off and the meat is cooked as usual.

Cures

As early as 12,000 years ago, our Neolithic ancestors discovered the application of salt could improve the texture and taste of meat, but more importantly, it retarded spoilage. (In the last century, we also learned it inhibits food-borne illnesses.) Today, humans still enjoy cured meats. Just look at the proliferation on menus of charcuterie boards, jaw-stretching pastrami sandwiches, not to mention our ongoing obsession with bacon, bacon, bacon!

Similar to brines, cures can be wet or dry. They usually contain high concentrations of salt as well as sodium nitrite, known in this book as pink curing salt #1 but often sold as Prague powder. Curing salt is deliberately dyed pink to distinguish it from other salts in your kitchen because it's toxic in high concentrations. (Don't confuse it with Himalayan salt, which also has a pinkish hue but not the same properties.) A few recipes in this book use cures, including home-cured bacon (page 80), beef jerky (page 40), and ham hocks (a.k.a. Pig on a Stick [page 88]). Measure curing salt accurately.

There was a bit of hysteria in the 1970s regarding nitrites. But they were unjustly accused. In fact, the USDA established a maximum of 156 parts per million (ppm) for cured meats, including hot dogs. That's a miniscule amount when you consider that such vegetables as lettuce, beets, celery, radishes, and carrots can contain as many as 1900 ppm. Roughly 93 percent of our nitrite intake comes from tubers and leafy vegetables.

Sauces, Rubs & Marinades

These staple recipes are great to have on hand to top your freshly grilled foods. Or for late-night snacks. Maybe a salad? You can use these for about anything! Really!

Smoked Tomato Sauce

2lb (1kg) Roma tomatoes, halved lengthwise

4 garlic cloves, impaled on a toothpick or wooden skewer

¼ cup extra virgin olive oil

1 large sweet white onion, peeled and diced

½ to 1 canned chipotle pepper in adobo sauce, plus more

2 tsp adobo sauce, plus more

1½ tbsp agave, light brown sugar, or low-carb substitute, plus more

½ tsp ground cumin

1 tsp coarse salt, plus more

1. Preheat the grill to 450°F (232°C).

2. Place the tomatoes cut sides down on the grate and balance the skewered garlic on the bars. Smoke for 30 minutes. Remove the tomatoes and garlic from the grill and coarsely chop.

3. In a small saucepan on the stovetop over medium heat, warm the olive oil. Add the onion and sauté until soft and lightly browned, about 6 to 8 minutes. Place the olive oil, onion, tomatoes, garlic, peppers and adobo sauce, agave, cumin, and salt in a blender. Pureé until smooth.

4. Taste and add more chipotle peppers and/or adobo sauce, agave, or salt if desired. Keep warm until serving. (The sauce can be made up to 1 day ahead. Cover and refrigerate. Rewarm before serving.)

White Barbecue Sauce

1 cup reduced-fat mayo

2 tbsp apple cider vinegar

2 tbsp horseradish

2 tbsp distilled water, plus more

1 tbsp freshly squeezed lemon juice

1 tbsp light brown sugar or low-carb substitute

1½ tsp hot sauce

1 tsp mustard powder

1 tsp coarse salt

½ tsp Worcestershire sauce

½ tsp ground cayenne

1. In a medium bowl, whisk the ingredients together until smooth. The sauce should be pourable and have good balance between tart and sweet. Adjust the flavors to suit your taste.

2. Cover and refrigerate until ready to use.

Horseradish Sauce

1½ cups light sour cream
½ cup reduced-fat mayo
¼ cup white horseradish, plus more
2 tbsp Dijon mustard
2 tsp Worcestershire sauce
coarse salt, plus more
freshly ground black pepper, plus more
2 tbsp minced fresh chives or flat-leaf parsley

1. In a medium bowl, combine the ingredients. Taste, adding more horseradish or salt and pepper as desired.

2. Cover and refrigerate until ready to use. (It will last for up to 2 days when refrigerated.)

Peanut Sauce

½ cup creamy peanut butter (preferably unsweetened), plus more
2 tbsp light soy sauce or liquid aminos
1 tbsp freshly squeezed lime juice, plus more
1 tbsp light brown sugar or low-carb substitute, plus more
1 tsp peeled and finely grated fresh ginger
1 tsp sriracha, plus more
1 to 4 tbsp Thai-style unsweetened coconut milk
chopped dry-roasted salted peanuts (optional)

1. In a blender, combine the peanut butter, soy sauce, lime juice, brown sugar, ginger, and sriracha. Blend until the sauce is smooth. Taste, adding more lime juice, brown sugar, or sriracha if desired. Add the coconut milk as needed to make a clingy but pourable sauce. If the sauce is too thin, add more peanut butter.

2. Transfer the sauce to a serving bowl and top with chopped peanuts (if using). Cover and refrigerate until ready to use. (It will last for up to 3 days when refrigerated.) Let the sauce come to room temperature before serving.

Ginger & Miso Dressing

¼ cup light soy sauce
2 tbsp distilled water
2 tbsp rice vinegar
1½ tbsp white or red miso
1 tbsp freshly squeezed lime juice
1 garlic clove, peeled and coarsely chopped
2 tsp peeled and minced fresh ginger
1 tsp Asian fish sauce (optional)
1 tbsp dark sesame oil
⅓ cup vegetable oil

1. In a blender, combine the soy sauce, water, vinegar, miso, lime juice, garlic, ginger, and fish sauce (if using). Blend until smooth.

2. With the machine running, slowly add the sesame and vegetable oils. Blend until the dressing is emulsified.

3. Cover and refrigerate until ready to serve.

Mustard Caviar

¼ cup yellow mustard seeds

¼ cup brown mustard seeds

1 cup distilled water

¼ cup apple cider vinegar

¼ cup apple cider or apple juice

¼ cup light brown sugar or low-carb substitute

2 tsp coarse salt

2 tsp Dijon mustard (optional)

1. In a jar with a tight-fitting lid, place the yellow and brown mustard seeds and the water. Refrigerate for 3 days, shaking the jar daily.

2. Drain the water from the mustard seeds. In a small saucepan on the stovetop over medium-high heat, combine the seeds, vinegar, apple cider, brown sugar, and salt. Bring the mixture to a boil. Reduce the heat to medium and simmer, watching carefully and stirring often, until most of the liquid has evaporated and the seeds "pop" like caviar when bitten into. (Add a bit more liquid if the caviar looks dry.) Stir in the Dijon mustard if you'd like the condiment to have a sharper taste.

3. Remove the saucepan from the stovetop and let the mixture cool. Transfer the mustard caviar to a covered jar and refrigerate until ready to use. (It will last for up to 2 weeks when refrigerated.)

Salsa de Molcajete

2 Roma tomatoes

2 tomatillos, husked and washed

1 jalapeño or serrano pepper

1 small white onion, halved

2 garlic cloves, peeled and impaled on a toothpick

½ tsp coarse salt, plus more

juice of ½ lime

¼ cup loosely packed fresh cilantro leaves

1. Preheat the grill to 450°F (232°C).

2. Place the tomatoes, tomatillos, jalapeño, and onion on the grate and balance the skewered garlic on the bars. Grill until they begin to char, about 3 minutes for the garlic and about 6 to 8 minutes for the other vegetables, turning as needed.

3. Transfer the vegetables to a rimmed sheet pan. Let them cool and then coarsely chop, leaving them in separate piles.

4. Place the garlic in a molcajete and add the salt. Mash the garlic to a purée using a temolote. Add the onion and grind it into the garlic paste, followed by the jalapeño (deseeded if desired for a milder salsa), tomatoes, and tomatillos.

5. Stir in the lime juice and cilantro. Taste for seasoning, adding more salt if necessary. Cover and refrigerate until ready to use. (If you don't own a molcajete or temolote, you can prepare the salsa in a food processor.)

Desert Island Barbecue Rub

This is the basic all-purpose barbecue rub I'd want if I were stranded on a desert island. It's compatible with pork, poultry, beef, and even vegetables. You probably have everything you need to make it in your pantry. (Make sure your spices are fresh so your rub is as vibrant as it can be.) Granulated brown sugar can be replaced with regular brown sugar, but I like the way the granulated variety mixes with the other spices without clumping.

Makes **about ¾ cup** • Prep time **5 mins**

¼ cup coarse salt

¼ cup granulated brown sugar or low-carb substitute

2 tbsp paprika

2 tbsp freshly ground black pepper

1 tbsp granulated garlic

2 tsp onion powder

2 tsp mustard powder

1 tsp celery salt

½ to 1 tsp ground cayenne

1. In a small bowl, whisk together the ingredients.

2. Store in an airtight container for up to 3 months.

Jalapeño Poppers
with Chipotle Sour Cream

Poppers wrapped in bacon can be awkward to eat one-handed, especially while standing. I prefer to blend crumbled bacon right into the filling. Serve these poppers with a chipotle-laced sour cream for a cooling counterpoint to the jalapeños' unpredictable heat.

oak or mesquite
WOOD PELLETS

375°F (191°C)
GRILL TEMP

40 to 45 mins
COOK TIME

Serves **8** • Prep time **20 mins** • Rest time **5 mins**

3 strips of thin-sliced bacon

12 large jalapeños, red, green, or a mix

8oz (225g) light cream cheese, at room temperature

1 cup shredded pepper Jack, Monterey Jack, or Cheddar cheese

1 tsp chili powder

½ tsp garlic salt

smoked paprika

for the sour cream

1¼ cups light sour cream

juice of ½ lime

½ to 1 canned chipotle peppers in adobo sauce, finely minced, plus 1 tsp of sauce, plus more

1 tbsp minced fresh cilantro leaves

½ tsp coarse salt, plus more

1. Preheat the grill to 375°F (191°C).

2. Line a rimmed sheet pan with aluminum foil and place a wire rack on top. Place the bacon in a single layer on the wire rack. Place the pan on the grate and grill until the bacon is crisp and golden brown, about 20 minutes. Transfer the bacon to paper towels to cool and then crumble. Set aside.

3. In a small bowl, make the chipotle sour cream by whisking together the ingredients. Add more salt, chipotle peppers, or adobe sauce to taste. Cover and refrigerate.

4. Slice the jalapeños lengthwise through their stems. Scrape out the veins and seeds with the edge of a small metal spoon.

5. In a small bowl, beat together the cream cheese, shredded cheese, chili powder, and garlic salt. Stir in the crumbled bacon. Mound the cream cheese mixture in the jalapeño halves. Line another rimmed sheet pan with aluminum foil and place a wire rack on top. Place the jalapeños filled side up in a single layer on the wire rack.

6. Place the sheet pan on the grate and roast the jalapeños until the filling has melted and the peppers have softened, about 20 to 25 minutes. (They should no longer look bright in color.) Remove the pan from the grill and let the peppers rest for 5 minutes.

7. Transfer the poppers to a platter and lightly dust with paprika. Serve with the chipotle sour cream.

TIPS | *Poppers are easily customizable. For variations, stir in diced crabmeat and fresh corn kernels; add minced scallions or chives; or substitute cooked chorizo or another sausage for bacon.*

Nutrition per 3 poppers
Calories **298** • Total fat **25g** • Carbs **5g** • Dietary fiber **1g** • Sugars **1g** • Protein **15g**

Roasted Red Pepper Dip

cherry or apple
WOOD PELLETS

400°F (204°C)
GRILL TEMP

40 to 45 mins
COOK TIME

Inspired by an appetizer that's popular in Turkey and Syria, this attractive dip—known as *muhammara*—features nutrient-packed red bell peppers and walnuts. Red bell peppers have 11 times the beta carotene and almost twice the vitamin C of their green counterparts.

Serves **8** • Prep time **20 mins** • Rest time **none**

4 red bell peppers, halved, destemmed, and deseeded

1 cup English walnuts, divided

1 small white onion, peeled and coarsely chopped

2 garlic cloves, peeled and smashed with a chef's knife

¼ cup extra virgin olive oil, plus more

1 tbsp balsamic vinegar or balsamic glaze

1 tsp honey (eliminate if using balsamic glaze)

1 tsp coarse salt, plus more

1 tsp ground cumin

1 tsp smoked paprika

½ to 1 tsp Aleppo red pepper flakes, plus more

¼ cup fresh white breadcrumbs (optional)

distilled water (optional)

assorted crudités or wedges of pita bread

1. Preheat the grill to 400°F (204°C).

2. Place the peppers skin side down on the grate and grill until the skins blister and the flesh softens, about 30 minutes. Transfer the peppers to a bowl and cover with plastic wrap. Let cool to room temperature. Remove the skins with a paring knife or your fingers. Coarsely chop or tear the peppers.

3. Place ¾ cup of walnuts in an aluminum foil roasting pan. Place the pan on the grate and toast for 10 to 15 minutes, stirring twice. Remove the pan from the grill and let the walnuts cool.

4. Place the peppers, onion, garlic, and walnuts in a food processor fitted with the chopping blade. Pulse several times. Add the olive oil, balsamic vinegar, honey, salt, cumin, paprika, and red pepper flakes. Process until the mixture is fairly smooth. Taste for seasoning, adding more salt or red pepper flakes (if desired). (If the mixture is too loose, add breadcrumbs until the texture is to your liking. If it's too thick, add olive oil or water 1 tablespoon at a time.)

5. Transfer the dip to a serving bowl. Use the back of a spoon to make a shallow depression in the center. Top with the remaining ¼ cup of walnuts and drizzle olive oil in the depression. Serve with crudités or pita bread.

TIPS | *This dip is traditionally made with pomegranate molasses, which can be difficult to find in some markets unless you're willing to shop online. Balsamic vinegar combined with honey makes a decent substitute, as does balsamic glaze, which is often found near the vinegar in many supermarkets. Leftovers can be served as a sauce for grilled meats or vegetables or as a spread for grilled bread. Cover and refrigerate the dip for up to 3 days.*

Nutrition per ¼ cup
Calories **161** • Total fat **15g** • Carbs **7g** • Dietary fiber **2g** • Sugars **2g** • Protein **3g**

Chicken Wings
with Teriyaki Glaze

cherry or maple
WOOD PELLETS

350°F (177°C)
GRILL TEMP

45 to 50 mins
COOK TIME

Americans love their chicken wings, consuming 1.35 billion on Super Bowl Sunday alone. If you like a little heat on your wings, add sriracha to the glaze. Authentic teriyaki glaze is quite thin, so this recipe comes with instructions for a thicker, glossier coating.

Serves **4** • Prep time **20 mins** • Rest time **none**

16 large chicken wings, about 3lb (1.4kg) total

1 to 1½ tbsp toasted sesame oil

for the glaze

½ cup light soy sauce or tamari

¼ cup sake or sugar-free dark-colored soda

¼ cup light brown sugar or low-carb substitute

2 tbsp mirin or 1 tbsp honey

1 garlic clove, peeled, minced or grated

2 tsp minced fresh ginger

1 tsp cornstarch mixed with 1 tbsp distilled water (optional)

for serving

1 tbsp toasted sesame seeds

2 scallions, trimmed, white and green parts sliced sharply diagonally

1. Preheat the grill to 350°F (177°C).

2. Place the chicken wings in a large bowl, add the sesame oil, and turn the wings to coat thoroughly.

3. Place the wings on the grate at an angle to the bars. Grill for 20 minutes and then turn. Continue to cook until the wings are nicely browned and the meat is no longer pink at the bone, about 20 minutes more.

4. To make the glaze, in a saucepan on the stovetop over medium-high heat, combine the ingredients and bring the mixture to a boil. Reduce the glaze by ⅓, about 6 to 8 minutes. If you prefer your glaze to be glossy and thick, add the cornstarch and water mixture to the glaze and cook until it coats the back of a spoon, about 1 to 2 minutes more.

5. Transfer the wings to an aluminum foil roasting pan. Pour the glaze over them, turning to coat thoroughly. Place the pan on the grate and cook the wings until the glaze sets, about 5 to 10 minutes.

6. Transfer the wings to a platter. Scatter the sesame seeds and scallions over the top. Serve with plenty of napkins.

TIP | To peel fresh ginger with the least amount of waste, use the edge of a metal teaspoon and scrape the thin skin off the ginger.

Nutrition per 4 wings

Calories **461** • Total fat **28g** • Carbs **11g** • Dietary fiber **0g** • Sugars **9g** • Protein **38g**

Grilled Guacamole

First enjoyed by the Aztecs, guacamole has become a popular snack in many parts of the world, with Americans eating 8 million pounds on Super Bowl Sunday alone. If you own a molcajete, you can make and serve the guacamole in this uniquely Latin American mortar bowl.

oak or mesquite
WOOD PELLETS

225°F (107°C)
GRILL TEMP

30 mins
COOK TIME

Serves **6** • Prep time **25 mins** • Rest time **none**

3 large avocados, halved and pitted

1 lime, halved

½ jalapeño, deseeded and deveined

½ small white or red onion, peeled

2 garlic cloves, peeled and skewered on a toothpick

1 tsp coarse salt, plus more

1½ tbsp reduced-fat mayo

2 tbsp chopped fresh cilantro

2 tbsp crumbled queso fresco (optional)

tortilla chips

1. Preheat the grill to 225°F (107°C).

2. Place the avocados, lime, jalapeño, and onion cut sides down on the grate. Use the toothpicks to balance the garlic cloves between the bars. Smoke for 30 minutes. (You want the vegetables to retain most of their rawness.)

3. Transfer everything to a cutting board. Remove the garlic cloves from the toothpick and roughly chop. Sprinkle with the salt and continue to mince the garlic until it begins to form a paste. Scrape the garlic and salt into a large bowl.

4. Scoop the avocado flesh from the peels into the bowl. Squeeze the juice of ½ lime over the avocado. Mash the avocados but leave them somewhat chunky. Finely dice the jalapeño. Dice 2 tablespoons of onion. (Reserve the remaining onion for another use.) Add the jalapeño, onion, mayo, and cilantro to the bowl. Stir gently to combine. Taste for seasoning, adding more salt, lime juice, and jalapeño as desired.

5. Transfer the guacamole to a serving bowl. Top with the queso fresco (if using). Serve with tortilla chips.

TIPS | *If you or your guests are watching carbs, serve thin slices of peeled jícama or kohlrabi as an alternative to tortilla chips. Although guacamole is best when made shortly before serving, it can be held for a few hours or overnight by using this trick: Place the guacamole in a lidded container. Slowly pour cool water over the top until the dip is covered by about ½ inch (1.25cm). When ready to serve, carefully pour off the water and restir the guacamole. The water protects the surface of the dip from air, preventing oxidation.*

Nutrition per ½ cup
Calories **235** • Total fat **23g** • Carbs **10g** • Dietary fiber **6g** • Sugars **2g** • Protein **1g**

Cold-Smoked Cheese

If your only experiences with smoked cheese came courtesy of holiday comestibles from the mall, you're in for a treat! Subtly flavored with real wood smoke, this cheese brings a cache to charcuterie or snack platters, sauces, sandwiches (especially grilled cheese), soups, salads, and more.

fruitwoods, alder, or hickory
WOOD PELLETS

0°F (0°C)
GRILL TEMP

1 to 3 hrs
COOK TIME

Makes **2lb (1kg)** • Prep time **10 mins** • Rest time **48 to 72 hrs**

2lb (1kg) well-chilled hard or semi-hard cheese, such as:
- Edam
- Gouda
- Cheddar
- Monterey Jack
- pepper Jack
- goat cheese
- fresh mozzarella
- Muenster
- aged Parmigiano-Reggiano
- Gruyère
- blue cheese

1. Unwrap the cheese and remove any protective wax or coating. Cut into 4-ounce (110g) portions to increase the surface area.

2. If possible, move your smoker to a shady area. Place 1 resealable plastic bag filled with ice on top of the drip pan. This is especially important on a warm day because you want to keep the interior temperature of the grill between 70 and 90°F (21 and 32°C) or below.

3. Place a grill mat on one side of the grate. Place the cheese on the mat and allow space between each piece.

4. Fill your smoking tube or pellet maze (see page 19) with pellets or sawdust and light according to the manufacturer's instructions. Place the smoking tube on the grate near—but not on—the grill mat. When the tube is smoking consistently, close the grill lid.

5. Smoke the cheese for 1 to 3 hours, replacing the pellets or sawdust and ice if necessary. Monitor the temperature and make sure the cheese isn't beginning to melt. Carefully lift the mat with the cheese to a rimmed baking sheet and let the cheese cool completely before handling.

6. Package the smoked cheese in cheese storage paper or bags or vacuum-seal the cheese, labeling each. (While you can wrap the cheese tightly in plastic wrap, the cheese will spoil faster.) Let the cheese rest for at least 2 to 3 days before eating. It will be even better after 2 weeks.

TIPS | *Cold-smoking works best in cooler weather. Don't oversmoke the cheese; 1 to 3 hours is enough to impart a pleasant flavor. Too much smoke and the cheese takes on an acrid taste.*

Nutrition per 2oz (55g)
Calories **240** • Total fat **20g** • Carbs **2g** • Dietary fiber **0g** • Sugars **0g** • Protein **13g**

Deviled Eggs
with Smoked Paprika

hickory
WOOD PELLETS

180°F (82°C)
GRILL TEMP

25 to 30 mins
COOK TIME

Once served at ancient Roman banquets, deviled eggs are popular in Europe and the United States. This smoked version makes a tangy and colorful accompaniment to barbecued meats. Starting the eggs in hot water results in eggs that peel easily and have perfectly cooked yolks.

Serves **6** • Prep time **25 mins** • Rest time **none**

6 large eggs

3 tbsp reduced-fat mayo, plus more

1 tsp Dijon or yellow mustard

½ tsp Spanish smoked paprika or regular paprika, plus more

dash of hot sauce

coarse salt

freshly ground black pepper

for garnishing
small sprigs of fresh parsley, dill, tarragon, or cilantro

chopped chives

minced scallions

Mustard Caviar (page 26)

sliced green or black olives

celery leaves

sliced radishes

diced bell peppers

sliced cherry tomatoes

fresh or pickled jalapeños

sliced or diced pickles

slivers of sun-dried tomatoes

bacon crumbles

smoked salmon

Hawaiian black salt

caviar

1. Preheat the grill to 180°F (82°C).

2. On the stovetop over medium-high heat, bring a saucepan of water to a boil. (Make sure there's enough water in the saucepan to cover the eggs by 1 inch [2.5cm].) Use a slotted spoon to gently lower the eggs into the water. Lower the heat to maintain a simmer. Set a timer for 13 minutes.

3. Prepare an ice bath by combining ice and cold water in a large bowl. Carefully transfer the eggs to the ice bath when the timer goes off.

4. When the eggs are cool enough to handle, gently tap them all over to crack the shell. Carefully peel the eggs. Rinse under cold running water to remove any clinging bits of shell, but don't dry the eggs. (A damp surface will help the smoke adhere to the egg whites.)

5. Place the eggs on the grate and smoke until the eggs take on a light brown patina from the smoke, about 25 minutes. Transfer the eggs to a cutting board, handling them as little as possible.

6. Slice each egg in half lengthwise with a sharp knife. Wipe any yolk off the blade before slicing the next egg. Gently remove the yolks and place them in a food processor. Pulse to break up the yolks. Add the mayo, mustard, paprika, and hot sauce. Season with salt and pepper to taste. Pulse until the filling is smooth. Add additional mayo 1 teaspoon at a time if the mixture is a little dry. (It shouldn't be too loose either.)

7. Spoon the filling into each egg half or pipe it in using a small resealable plastic bag. You can also use a pastry bag fitted with a fluted tip.

8. Place the eggs on a platter and lightly dust with paprika. Accompany with one or more of the suggested garnishes.

Nutrition per 2 egg halves
Calories **120** • Total fat **10g** • Carbs **1g** • Dietary fiber **0g** • Sugars **1g** • Protein **7g**

Sriracha & Maple Cashews

maple
WOOD PELLETS

250°F (121°C)
GRILL TEMP

1 hr
COOK TIME

I discovered this addictive flavor combination—sriracha, maple syrup, and butter—one snowy January day when a trip to the grocery store was out of the question. I debuted it on chicken drumsticks but discovered I like it even better on cashews. These would make a great gift for holidays or birthdays.

Serves **10** • Prep time **5 mins** • Rest time **15 mins**

2 tbsp unsalted butter

3 tbsp pure maple syrup

1 tbsp sriracha

1 tsp coarse salt (use only if nuts are unsalted)

2½ cups unsalted cashews

1. Preheat the grill to 250°F (121°C).

2. In a small saucepan on the stovetop over low heat, melt the butter. Add the maple syrup, sriracha, and salt (if using). Stir until combined. Add the nuts and stir gently to coat thoroughly.

3. Spread the nuts in a single layer in an aluminum foil roasting pan coated with cooking spray. Place the pan on the grate and smoke the nuts until they're lightly toasted, about 1 hour, stirring once or twice.

4. Remove the pan from the grill and let the nuts cool for 15 minutes. They'll be sticky at first but will crisp up. Break them up with your fingers and store at room temperature in an airtight container, such as a lidded glass jar.

TIPS | *Feel free to substitute other nuts for the cashews, such as pecans, almonds, and mixed nuts. They make great gifts.*

Nutrition per ¼ cup
Calories **223** • Total fat **17g** • Carbs **14g** • Dietary fiber **1g** • Sugars **6g** • Protein **6g**

Citrus-Infused Marinated Olives

olive or pecan
WOOD PELLETS

180°F (82°C)
GRILL TEMP

30 mins
COOK TIME

For this colorful appetizer, use a mix of brine-cured table olives, such as Cerignola, Castelvetrano, Kalamata, or Picholine. Also, if you're unfamiliar with smoked Spanish paprika—also known as *pimentón*—it's usually available in the spice aisle or you can purchase it online.

Serves **6** • Prep time **15 mins** • Rest time **none**

1½ cups mixed brined olives, with pits

½ cup extra virgin olive oil

1 tbsp freshly squeezed lemon juice

1 garlic clove, peeled and thinly sliced

1 tsp smoked Spanish paprika

2 sprigs of fresh rosemary

2 sprigs of fresh thyme

2 bay leaves, fresh or dried

1 small dried red chili pepper, deseeded and flesh crumbled, or ¼ tsp crushed red pepper flakes

3 strips of orange zest

3 strips of lemon zest

1. Preheat the grill to 180°F (82°C).

2. Drain the olives, reserving 1 tablespoon of brine. Spread the olives in a single layer in an aluminum foil roasting pan. Place the pan on the grate and cook the olives for 30 minutes, stirring the olives or shaking the pan once or twice.

3. In a small saucepan on the stovetop over low heat, warm the olive oil. Whisk in the lemon juice and the reserved 1 tablespoon of brine. Stir in the garlic and paprika. Add the rosemary, thyme, bay leaves, chili pepper, and orange and lemon zests. Warm over low heat for 10 minutes. Remove the saucepan from the heat.

4. Transfer the olives and olive oil mixture to a pint jar. Tuck the aromatics around the sides of the jar. Let cool and then cover and refrigerate for up to 5 days. Let the olives come to room temperature before serving.

TIPS | *A single-edged razor blade works even better than a small knife when slicing garlic cloves. Smoked olives look jewel-like on a charcuterie platter. Be sure to provide guests with cocktail napkins and a small dish for olive pits.*

Nutrition per ¼ cup
Calories **171** • Total fat **18g** • Carbs **4g** • Dietary fiber **0g** • Sugars **0g** • Protein **0g**

Chuckwagon Beef Jerky

Jerky is one of the fastest-growing segments of the snack food industry. Low in calories and fat and high in protein, jerky is an egalitarian nibble that's sold at gas stations and high-end gourmet retailers alike. But there's nothing like homemade jerky. It's addictive!

oak or mesquite
WOOD PELLETS

150°F (66°C)
GRILL TEMP

4 to 5 hrs
COOK TIME

Makes **1lb (450g)** • Prep time **20 mins** • Rest time **30 mins**

2½lb (1.2kg) boneless top or bottom round steak, sirloin tip, flank steak, or venison

1 cup sugar-free dark-colored soda

1 cup cold brewed coffee

½ cup light soy sauce

¼ cup Worcestershire sauce

2 tbsp whiskey (optional)

2 tsp chili powder

1½ tsp garlic salt

1 tsp onion powder

1 tsp pink curing salt #1 (optional)

1. Slice the meat into ¼-inch-thick (.5cm) strips, trimming off any visible fat or gristle. (Slice against the grain for more tender jerky and with the grain for chewier jerky.) Place the meat in a large resealable plastic bag.

2. In a small bowl, whisk together the soda, coffee, soy sauce, Worcestershire sauce, whiskey (if using), chili powder, garlic salt, onion powder, and curing salt (if using). Whisk until the salt dissolves. Pour the mixture over the meat and reseal the bag. Refrigerate for 24 to 48 hours, turning the bag several times to redistribute the brine.

3. Preheat the grill to 150°F (66°C).

4. Drain the meat and discard the brine. Place the strips of meat in a single layer on paper towels and blot any excess moisture.

5. Place the meat in a single layer on the grate and smoke for 4 to 5 hours, turning once or twice. (If you're aware of hot spots on your grate, rotate the strips so they smoke evenly.) To test for doneness, bend one or two pieces in the middle. They should be dry but still somewhat pliant. Or simply eat a piece to see if it's done to your liking.

6. For the best texture, when you remove the meat from the grill, place the still-warm jerky in a resealable plastic bag and let rest for 30 minutes. (You might see condensation form on the inside of the bag, but the moisture will be reabsorbed by the meat.) Or let the meat cool completely and then store in a resealable plastic bag or covered container. The jerky will last a few days at room temperature but will last longer (up to 2 weeks) if refrigerated.

TIPS | *The meat is easier to slice thinly if you partially freeze it for 30 to 40 minutes.*

Nutrition per 2oz (55g)
Calories **222** • Total fat **6g** • Carbs **4g** • Dietary fiber **1g** • Sugars **2g** • Protein **36g**

Bayou Wings
with Cajun Rémoulade

While I typically like to brine chicken in a saltwater solution before grilling, using a rub containing salt (called dry-brining) also adds moisture and flavor if applied in advance. Exposing the wings to higher heat will help brown and crisp the skin. And the rémoulade complements the enhanced flavors of the rub.

pecan
WOOD PELLETS

350°F (177°C)
GRILL TEMP

40 mins
COOK TIME

Serves **8** • Prep time **15 mins** • Rest time **none**

16 large whole chicken wings or 32 drumettes and flats, about 3lb (1.4kg) total

for the rub
1 tbsp kosher salt
1 tsp freshly ground black pepper
1 tsp paprika
½ tsp ground cayenne, plus more
½ tsp garlic powder
½ tsp celery salt
½ tsp dried thyme
2 tbsp vegetable oil

for the rémoulade
1¼ cups reduced-fat mayo
¼ cup Creole-style or whole grain mustard
2 tbsp horseradish
2 tbsp pickle relish
1 tbsp freshly squeezed lemon juice
1 tsp paprika, plus more
1 tsp hot sauce, plus more
1 tsp Worcestershire sauce
coarse salt

for serving
lemon wedges
pickled okra (optional)

1. Preheat the grill to 350°F (177°C).

2. If using whole wings, cut through the two joints, separating them into drumettes, flats, and wing tips. (Discard the wing tips or save them for chicken stock.) Alternatively, leave the wings whole. Place the chicken in a resealable plastic bag.

3. In a small bowl, make the rub by combining the ingredients. Mix well. Pour the rub over the wings and toss them to thoroughly coat. Refrigerate for 2 hours.

4. In a small bowl, make the Cajun rémoulade by whisking together the mayo, mustard, horseradish, pickle relish, lemon juice, paprika, hot sauce, and Worcestershire. Season with salt to taste. The mixture should be highly seasoned. Transfer to a serving bowl and lightly dust with paprika. Cover and refrigerate until ready to serve.

5. Remove the wings from the refrigerator and allow the excess marinade to drip off. Place the wings on the grate at an angle to the bars. Grill for 20 minutes and then turn. (They'll brown more evenly but will also have less of a tendency to stick.) Continue to cook until the wings are nicely browned and the meat is no longer pink at the bone, about 20 minutes more.

6. Remove the wings from the grill and pile them on a platter. Serve with the Cajun rémoulade, lemon wedges, and pickled okra (if using).

TIPS | *You can easily substitute jumbo shrimp, peeled and deveined, for the wings. Refrigerate for 15 to 30 minutes after applying the rub/dry brine. Grill at 400°F (204°C) until opaque and just firm, about 3 to 4 minutes per side.*

Nutrition per 2 whole wings or 4 drumettes and/or flats
Calories **855** • Total fat **77g** • Carbs **0g** • Dietary fiber **1g** • Sugars **0g** • Protein **37g**

BEEF,
LAMB
& GAME

Marinated Flank Steak

Contrary to popular belief, marinades add flavor but do little to tenderize tougher belly cuts like flank steak because they only penetrate the meat by about ¼ inch (.5cm). Slicing thinly on a sharp diagonal against the grain will shorten the fibers, making the steak seem more tender.

oak, pecan, or hickory
WOOD PELLETS

450°F (232°C)
GRILL TEMP

8 to 10 mins
COOK TIME

Serves **6** • Prep time **10 mins** • Rest time **5 mins**

2lb (1kg) flank steak
coarse salt
freshly ground black pepper

for the marinade
¼ cup red wine vinegar
2 tbsp Worcestershire sauce
1½ tsp coarse salt
½ cup extra virgin olive oil
2 garlic cloves, peeled and smashed with a chef's knife
1 small white onion, coarsely chopped
2 tbsp finely chopped fresh rosemary leaves
sprigs of fresh rosemary

1. In a jar with a tight-fitting lid, make the marinade by combining the vinegar, Worcestershire sauce, salt, and olive oil. Shake vigorously. Stir in the garlic, onion, and rosemary leaves.

2. Place the flank steak in a resealable plastic bag and pour the marinade over it. Turn the steak to thoroughly coat. Refrigerate for 8 to 24 hours, turning the bag periodically to thoroughly marinate the steak.

3. Preheat the grill to 450°F (232°C).

4. Remove the steak from the marinade and pat dry with paper towels. (Discard the marinade.) Season on both sides with salt and pepper.

5. Place the steak on the grate and grill until the internal temperature reaches 125 to 135°F (52 to 54°C), about 4 to 5 minutes per side.

6. Remove the steak from the grill and let rest for 5 minutes. Slice thinly against the grain with a knife held on a sharp diagonal. Transfer the slices to a platter and scatter rosemary sprigs over the top before serving.

TIPS | *If your grate doesn't produce good grill marks, place a cast iron grill pan on the grate before preheating your grill. You can also use an accessory like GrillGrates (see page 19).*

Nutrition per 5oz (140g)
Calories **345** • Total fat **21g** • Carbs **1g** • Dietary fiber **0g** • Sugars **1g** • Protein **37g**

Naked Juicy Lucy Burgers
with Special Sauce

hickory, oak, or pecan
WOOD PELLETS

225°F (107°C);
450°F (232°C)
GRILL TEMP

35 to 40 mins
COOK TIME

It's a tale of two cities: Dueling establishments on the south side of Minneapolis (my former hometown) claim their cheese-stuffed hamburgers are the original Juicy Lucys. The special sauce might seem familiar, but it's inspired by a now-defunct Denver-based burger chain called Rockybilt.

Serves **4** · Prep time **15 mins** · Rest time **3 mins**

2lb (1kg) ground beef (80/20), preferably chuck, well chilled

1 tbsp Worcestershire sauce or liquid aminos

6oz (170g) grated Cheddar, pepper Jack, or another melting cheese

coarse salt

freshly ground black pepper

for the sauce
¼ cup reduced-fat mayo
¼ cup yellow mustard
¼ cup ketchup
¼ cup Heinz 57 sauce
2 tbsp sweet pickle relish

for serving
sliced tomatoes
sliced sweet onions
lettuce leaves
cooked bacon strips
pickles

1. Preheat the grill to 225°F (107°C).

2. In a small bowl, make the sauce by combining the ingredients. Transfer the sauce to a serving bowl. Cover and refrigerate until ready to use. (Leftover sauce will keep for several weeks.)

3. Place the ground beef in a large bowl and add the Worcestershire sauce. Wet your hands with cold water and lightly mix. Divide the mixture into 8 equal-sized balls. Flatten each ball into a round patty.

4. Place 4 patties on a rimmed sheet pan. Mound an equal amount of cheese in the middle of each patty, leaving a meat border. Place a patty on top of each cheese mound. Rewet your hands with cold water and press and pinch the edges of patties together to form a tight seal. (You don't want the cheese to leak out.) Season on both sides with salt and pepper.

5. Place the patties on the grate and smoke for 30 minutes. Transfer the burgers to a clean plate.

6. Raise the temperature to 450°F (232°C). Return the burgers to the grate and sear them until the burgers reach an internal temperature of 160°F (71°C), about 3 to 4 minutes per side, turning once.

7. Transfer the burgers to a platter and let rest for 3 minutes. Serve with the special sauce and the suggested accompaniments.

TIPS | *Stuff the burgers with **Cold-Smoked Cheese** (page 35). You can also use the above recipe to make sliders. Make about 2 per guest.*

Nutrition per 1 burger
Calories **442** · Total fat **34g** · Carbs **6g** · Dietary fiber **0g** · Sugars **5g** · Protein **29g**

Salt & Pepper Dinosaur Bones

hickory, oak, or mesquite
WOOD PELLETS

250°F (121°C)
GRILL TEMP

7 to 8 hrs
COOK TIME

Some pitmasters call these Flintstone-esque bones "brisket on a stick" because they're some of the meatiest, beefiest ribs you'll ever taste. Cut from the short plate, each rib usually weighs more than a pound and can be found at some big box stores and specialty butcher shops.

Serves **3 to 4** • Prep time **15 mins** • Rest time **1 hr**

1 rack of beef plate short ribs, about 4 to 5lb (1.8 to 2.3kg) total, or 3 bones

coarse kosher salt

freshly ground black pepper

granulated garlic

crushed red pepper flakes (optional)

1½ cups sugar-free dark-colored soda, sugar-free root beer, beef broth, or brewed coffee

1. Preheat the grill to 250°F (121°C).

2. Place the ribs in an aluminum foil roasting pan. If the rack has a thick cap of fat on the meaty side, trim most of it off because that will impede the formation of a nice bark on the ribs.

3. Generously season the ribs on all sides with salt, pepper, garlic, and red pepper flakes (if using). Place the ribs bone side down on the grate and smoke for 3 hours.

4. Add the soda to a spray bottle and spritz the ribs. Continue to smoke the ribs until the internal temperature reaches 203°F (95°C), about 4 to 5 hours more, spritzing once an hour. (Insert the probe next to the middle rib, being careful not to touch the bone.) When the ribs are tender, the meat will feel gelatinous and springy and will have shrunk back from the ends of the bones by up to 2 inches (5cm).

5. Transfer the ribs to a clean sheet pan and wrap with heavy-duty aluminum foil. Let rest for 1 hour, preferably in an insulated cooler.

6. Slice the ribs apart or remove the meat from the bones and thinly slice before serving with additional salt and pepper.

Nutrition per 6oz (170g)
Calories **1064** • Total fat **61g** • Carbs **2g** • Dietary fiber **0g** • Sugars **0g** • Protein **115g**

Roasted Prime Rib

Nothing says "special occasion" like prime rib—that baronial hunk of meat often appearing on holiday tables. Indulgent? Yes. But well worth the investment when you carve off that first succulent rosy-hued slice. I once found prime rib intimidating—but not with the wood pellet grill.

hickory or oak
WOOD PELLETS

450°F (232°C);
350°F (177°C)
GRILL TEMP

90 to 105 mins
COOK TIME

Serves **8** • Prep time **25 mins** • Rest time **15 mins**

1 four-bone prime rib roast, about 8lb (3.6kg), trimmed

extra virgin olive oil

1 cup beef stock or broth

fresh coarsely ground black pepper

Horseradish Sauce (page 28)

for the seasoned salt

¼ cup coarsely chopped fresh rosemary leaves

5 fresh sage leaves, coarsely chopped

1 tbsp granulated garlic or 2 tsp garlic powder

2 tsp whole black peppercorns or fresh coarsely ground black pepper

1¼ cups coarse salt, divided

1. Preheat the grill to 450°F (232°C).

2. In a coffee grinder, make the seasoned salt by combining the rosemary, sage, granulated garlic, peppercorns, and ½ cup of salt. Pulse until the herbs and peppercorns are finely ground and the coarse salt resembles table salt. (The mixture will be damp from the moisture in the herbs.)

3. Transfer the mixture to a bowl and stir in the remaining ¾ cup of salt. Reserve 3 to 4 teaspoons of the seasoned salt for the prime rib. Spread the remaining mixture on a rimmed sheet pan and let dry completely, stirring occasionally, before storing at room temperature in a covered jar. Set aside. (Place the mixture in a dehydrator or low-temperature oven or your smoker to hasten the drying time.)

4. Carve the bones off the roast in a single slab. Set aside. Use butcher's twine to tie the roast at 1½-inch (3.75cm) intervals. Lightly coat on all sides with olive oil and season with the reserved seasoned salt.

5. Place the bones convex (rounded) side up in an aluminum foil roasting pan. Place the prime rib atop the bones. Add the beef stock to the bottom of the pan.

6. Place the pan on the grate and roast until the exterior is nicely browned, about 30 minutes. Lower the temperature to 350°F (177°C) and continue to roast the meat until the internal temperature reaches 125°F (52°C) to 130°F (54°C), about 60 to 75 minutes, basting with the drippings every 20 minutes. (To avoid overcooking, check the internal temperature of the roast every 20 minutes.)

7. Transfer the roast to a cutting board and loosely tent with aluminum foil. Let rest for 15 minutes. Carve the prime rib into ¾-inch (2cm) slices and serve with the horseradish sauce.

Nutrition per 3oz (170g)
Calories **772** • Total fat **77g** • Carbs **4g** • Dietary fiber **1g** • Sugars **1g** • Protein **38g**

Chuck Roast Burnt Ends

Burnt ends were fatty chunks of beef brisket that were too overcooked to sell. So Arthur Bryant's in Kansas City began giving them away to customers who waited for their orders. Today, they're delectable bites of tender double-smoked meat enrobed in sticky KC-style barbecue sauce.

hickory or oak
WOOD PELLETS

250°F (121°C)
GRILL TEMP

6 to 8 hrs
COOK TIME

Serves **4** • Prep time **15 mins** • Rest time **10 mins**

1 chuck roast, about 3 to 4lb (1.4 to 1.8kg)

2 tbsp Worcestershire sauce, plus more

coarse salt, plus more

freshly ground black pepper, plus more

granulated garlic, plus more

1 cup low-carb barbecue sauce

¼ cup sugar-free dark-colored soda, plus more

1. Preheat the grill to 250°F (121°C).

2. Place the roast on a rimmed sheet pan and brush with the Worcestershire sauce. Lightly season with salt, pepper, and granulated garlic. Place the roast on the grate and smoke until the internal temperature reaches 170°F (77°C), about 5 to 6 hours.

3. Transfer the roast to a cutting board and let rest for 10 minutes. (Leave the grill going.) Use a sharp knife to slice the meat into bite-size cubes, trimming any excess fat if necessary. Place the meat in an aluminum foil roasting pan. Lightly season with more salt, pepper, and granulated garlic and toss the cubes with your hands to distribute the seasonings. Add the barbecue sauce and soda. Toss again to coat.

4. Place the pan on the grate and smoke until the meat is tender and somewhat sticky with sauce, about 1 to 2 hours, stirring occasionally. (Don't let the sauce scorch.) Add another splash of soda if needed.

5. Remove the pan from the grill and stir the meat again before serving.

TIPS | *Look for a chuck roast that exhibits nice marbling in the meat itself—not thick seams of fat. Serve the burnt ends with coleslaw, pickles, or baked beans (but watch the carbs).*

Nutrition per 6oz (170g)
Calories **502** • Total fat **14g** • Carbs **15g** • Dietary fiber **0g** • Sugars **6g** • Protein **78g**

Lamb Chops
with Lemon Vinaigrette

hickory or oak
WOOD PELLETS

450°F (232°C)
GRILL TEMP

12 to 16 mins
COOK TIME

Supernaturally tender and mild flavored, lamb rib chops are spectacular when grilled over high heat and drizzled with a tangy vinaigrette. For a more elegant presentation, ask your butcher to "french" the bones—that is, clean them of excess fat and bits of meat.

Serves **4** • Prep time **15 mins** • Rest time **3 mins**

8 lamb rib chops, about 2lb (1kg) total and each about ¾ inch (2cm) thick

3 tbsp extra virgin olive oil

coarse salt

freshly ground black pepper

for the vinaigrette

4 lemons, halved

1 tbsp plus 1 cup extra virgin olive oil, plus more

4 large basil leaves, coarsely chopped

1 garlic clove, peeled and coarsely chopped

1 tsp Dijon mustard

1 tsp honey

1 tsp coarse salt

½ tsp freshly ground black pepper, plus more

1. Preheat the grill to 450°F (232°C).

2. Coat the lamb chops on each side with the olive oil. Season with salt and pepper. (For the best crust, do this 45 minutes before grilling.)

3. Begin making the vinaigrette by brushing the lemon halves with 1 tablespoon of olive oil. Place the halves cut sides down on the grate and grill until they exhibit some charring, about 6 to 8 minutes. Transfer the lemons to a bowl and let cool.

4. Juice 4 lemon halves through a strainer positioned over a blender. (Reserve the remaining lemon halves for garnishing.) Add the basil leaves, garlic, mustard, honey, and salt and pepper to the blender. Add ¼ cup of olive oil and blend until the garlic is minced and everything's well combined. While the machine's running, slowly add the remaining ¾ cup of olive oil. Taste for seasoning, adding more salt. (If the dressing is too tart, add a little more honey or olive oil—the latter 1 tablespoon at a time.) Transfer the vinaigrette to a pitcher or a cruet.

5. Place the lamb chops on the still-hot grate at an angle to the bars. Grill until the chops have grill marks and the internal temperature reaches 125 to 135°F (52 to 57°C), about 3 to 4 minutes per side.

6. Transfer the chops to a platter and let rest for 3 minutes. Drizzle the lemon vinaigrette over the top. Place 1 reserved lemon half on each plate before serving.

Nutrition per 2 chops

Calories **399** • Total fat **22g** • Carbs **0g** • Dietary fiber **0g** • Sugars **0g** • Protein **48g**

Texas Hill Country Brisket
with Mustard Barbecue Sauce

oak or mesquite
WOOD PELLETS

250°F (121°C)
GRILL TEMP

11 to 14 hrs
COOK TIME

It might seem odd to envision Texas Hill Country brisket with a South Carolina–style mustard barbecue sauce—that is, until you remember that mustard-loving German immigrants settled both areas in the 19th century. You can skip the sauce entirely, as many Texas pitmasters do.

Serves **10 to 12** • Prep time **20 mins** • Rest time **1 to 2 hrs**

1 whole packer brisket, about 12 to 14lb (5.4 to 6.4kg)

for the sauce
½ cup yellow mustard
½ cup brown mustard
½ cup apple cider vinegar
¼ cup light brown sugar or low-carb substitute, plus more
1 tbsp ketchup
1 tbsp Worcestershire sauce
1 tbsp hot sauce
1 tsp beef bouillon granules
1 tsp granulated garlic
1 tsp coarse salt, plus more
½ tsp freshly ground black pepper

for the rub
¼ cup coarse salt
¼ cup fresh coarsely ground black pepper
1 tbsp granulated garlic
1 tbsp chili powder

1. Place a pan of water on the grate. Preheat the grill to 250°F (121°C).

2. In a medium saucepan on the stovetop over medium-low heat, make the sauce by whisking together the ingredients. Bring the mixture to a simmer, stirring occasionally. Simmer for 10 minutes. Taste, adding brown sugar or salt. Transfer the sauce to a covered jar and refrigerate until ready to use.

3. In a small bowl, make the rub by combining the ingredients. Trim some of the excess exterior fat off the brisket, leaving a cap of at least ¼ inch (.5cm). Place the brisket on a rimmed baking sheet. Evenly but conservatively season the meat on all sides with the rub.

4. Place the brisket fat side down on the grate and smoke until the internal temperature reaches 165°F (74°C), about 5 to 6 hours.

5. Remove the brisket from the grill and wrap it fat side up in unlined butcher paper, crimping the seams. (You can also use aluminum foil—many well-known Texas pitmasters do—but it's not as porous.) Return the brisket seam side up to the grate. Continue to cook until the internal temperature reaches 203°F (95°C), about 6 to 8 hours more. The meat should be very tender, with the melted collagen making it almost jiggly.

6. Transfer the brisket to an insulated cooler lined with clean towels or a thick layer of newspapers. Let the meat rest for 1 to 2 hours.

7. Place the brisket on a cutting board and unwrap it. Separate the point from the flat following the seam of fat that runs between them. Use a serrated knife to slice the meat against the grain into pencil-thick pieces. (The grain in the point runs perpendicular to the grain in the flat.)

8. Shingle the meat on a platter. Drizzle with any meat juices from the cutting board. Serve with the barbecue sauce.

Nutrition per 6oz (170g)
Calories **662** • Total fat **28g** • Carbs **7g** • Dietary fiber **1g** • Sugars **5g** • Protein **96g**

Kalbi-Style Steak Wraps

Anyone interested in healthy grilling should look to Asian grillmasters, who tend to emphasize visually appealing, bright-tasting condiments accompanied by a relatively small quantity of meat. The marinade is also great for short ribs, pork tenderloin, or chicken breasts or thighs.

cherry
WOOD PELLETS

450°F (232°C)
GRILL TEMP

6 to 8 mins
COOK TIME

Serves **4** • Prep time **20 mins** • Rest time **2 mins**

1 flat iron steak, about 1½lb (680g)

1 tbsp toasted sesame seeds

2 scallions, trimmed, white and green parts thinly sliced on a sharp diagonal

for the marinade

1 small white onion, peeled and coarsely grated

4 garlic cloves, peeled and smashed with a chef's knife

½ Asian pear, decored and coarsely grated

½ cup light soy sauce

½ cup low-carb beer or distilled water

2 tbsp light brown sugar or low-carb substitute

2 tbsp rice vinegar or apple cider vinegar

2 tbsp toasted sesame oil

1 tbsp peeled and grated fresh ginger

1 tsp freshly ground black pepper

1. In a large bowl, make the marinade by combining the ingredients. Stir until the sugar dissolves. Place the steaks in a resealable plastic bag and add the marinade, massaging the bag to thoroughly coat the meat. Refrigerate for 8 hours or overnight, turning the bag once or twice.

2. Place a ridged cast iron grill pan or griddle on the grate. Preheat the grill to 450°F (232°C).

3. Remove the steaks from the marinade and remove any solids. (Discard the marinade.) Pat dry with paper towels. Place the steaks on the cast iron pan and grill until the internal temperature reaches 125 to 130°F (52 to 54°C), about 3 to 4 minutes per side, turning once.

4. Transfer the steaks to a cutting board and let rest for 2 minutes. Thinly slice each steak on a sharp diagonal and place on a platter. Scatter the sesame seeds and scallions over the top.

5. Place leaf lettuce, thinly sliced jalapeños, fresh cilantro leaves, kimchi (optional), and thinly sliced garlic on a separate platter. Place gochujang (Korean chili paste) in a small ramekin and add that to the platter.

6. Place the two platters on the table. Advise each diner to assemble the lettuce wraps to their desire. Serve with Asian beer, sake, or Korean soju.

TIPS | *Asian pears can be found in many US supermarkets. If they're not available, substitute another species of pear or even an apple, such as Fuji or Pink Lady. Do as chefs do: Use a single-edged industrial razor blade instead of a knife blade to thinly slice garlic cloves.*

Nutrition per 6oz (170g)

Calories **360** • Total fat **19g** • Carbs **6g** • Dietary fiber **1g** • Sugars **3g** • Protein **39g**

Bistro Steaks
with Avocado Relish

This is a steak with many aliases: bistro steak, petite shoulder tender, mock tender, and others. Its official name is teres major and it's cut from the shoulder clod. Usually weighing a bit less than a pound, this tender and economical steak resembles a mini tenderloin.

mesquite or oak
WOOD PELLETS

**180°F (82°C);
450°F (232°C)**
GRILL TEMP

34 mins
COOK TIME

Serves **4** • Prep time **20 mins** • Rest time **3 mins**

2lb (1kg) bistro steaks

extra virgin olive oil

liquid aminos

for the rub

2 tsp coarse salt

2 tsp fresh coarsely ground black pepper

2 tsp light brown sugar or low-carb substitute

2 tsp chili powder

2 tsp ground cumin

2 tsp granulated garlic

2 tsp sweet or smoked paprika

for the relish

2 avocados

1½ tbsp freshly squeezed lime juice, plus more

2 garlic cloves, peeled and finely minced

1 Roma tomato, decored, deseeded, and diced

1 jalapeño, destemmed, deseeded, and finely diced

¼ cup coarsely chopped fresh cilantro leaves

2 tbsp diced red onion

1 tbsp mayo

1 tsp hot sauce

coarse salt

1. Preheat the grill to 180°F (82°C).

2. In a small bowl, make the rub by combining the ingredients.

3. Trim any silver skin from the steaks and place them on a rimmed sheet pan. Coat with olive oil. Dust with the rub, patting it on with your fingertips.

4. Place the steaks on the grate and grill until the internal temperature reaches 110 to 115°F (43 to 46°C), about 30 minutes. Pour some liquid aminos into a small spray bottle and spritz the steaks before wrapping them in heavy-duty aluminum foil. Let the steaks rest.

5. Cut the avocados in half and then pit, peel, and dice them. In a medium bowl, make the relish by combining the avocado and lime juice. Add the remaining ingredients and season with salt to taste. Use a rubber spatula to gently mix. Transfer to an attractive serving bowl. Cover and refrigerate. (The relish is best if not made more than 1 hour ahead.)

6. Raise the temperature to 450°F (232°C). Remove the steaks from the foil and place them on the grate. Sear until they're browned and the internal temperature reaches 130 to 135°F (54 to 57°C), about 2 minutes per side, turning with tongs.

7. Transfer the steaks to a cutting board and let rest for 3 minutes. Slice them crosswise on a diagonal into ⅜-inch (1cm) slices. Shingle the slices on a platter and pour any juices remaining on the cutting board over the meat. Serve with the avocado relish.

Nutrition per 8oz (225g)

Calories **680** • Total fat **44g** • Carbs **10g** • Dietary fiber **9g** • Sugars **5g** • Protein **54g**

Tomahawk Steaks
with Garlic Herb Butter

Massive bone-in ribeye steaks, often sold as "tomahawk" or "cowboy," will make any card-carrying carnivore swoon. Identified by their long handle-like bone, they can weigh as much as 2.5 pounds (1kg) each. A simple compound butter applied after grilling lets the meat shine.

Serves **8** • Prep time **15 mins** • Rest time **3 mins**

hickory, oak, or pecan
WOOD PELLETS

225°F (107°C); 450°F (232°C)
GRILL TEMP

56 to 68 mins
COOK TIME

2 bone-in ribeye steaks, each about 1½ to 2lb (680g to 1kg)

coarse salt

fresh coarsely ground black pepper

for the butter

1 stick unsalted butter, at room temperature

1 to 2 garlic cloves, peeled and minced

1 tbsp minced fresh chives or scallion greens

1 tbsp minced fresh parsley

1 tsp freshly squeezed lemon juice

½ tsp coarse salt

½ tsp freshly ground black pepper

1. Preheat the grill to 225°F (107°C).

2. In a small bowl, make the herb butter by blending together the ingredients with a fork. Use wax paper, parchment paper, or plastic wrap as an aid to form the butter into a log and twist the ends of the wrapping. Chill in the refrigerator or freezer until ready to use.

3. Generously season the steaks with salt and pepper. Place them on the cast iron pan and grill until the internal temperature reaches 115°F (46°C), about 50 to 60 minutes. (Insert the probe through the side of a steak toward the center. Don't let the probe touch bone or you'll get an elevated reading.) Transfer the steaks to a rimmed baking sheet and cover loosely with aluminum foil.

4. Place a ridged cast iron grill pan or a set of GrillGrates on the grate. Raise the temperature to 450°F (232°C). Place the steaks on the cast iron pan and sear until the internal temperature reaches 130°F (54°C), about 3 to 4 minutes per side, turning once.

5. Transfer the steaks to a cutting board. Cut the butter into discs and place 3 or 4 atop each steak. Let the steaks rest for 3 minutes. If desired, cut the ribeyes off their bones and slice the meat. Reassemble the meat and bones on a platter before serving.

TIPS | *Double the recipe for the garlic herb butter. (If well wrapped, it will last for months in the freezer.) Use on vegetables, such as asparagus, carrots, corn, potatoes, or green beans. Keep the steaks refrigerated until you're ready to smoke and grill them. Yes, you've heard you should bring them to room temperature. But pricey steakhouses always keep their meats chilled.*

Nutrition per 8oz (225g)

Calories **664** • Total fat **58g** • Carbs **0g** • Dietary fiber **0g** • Sugars **0g** • Protein **30g**

Italian Meatballs

Some pitmasters refer to these smoked meatballs as "moink" balls—as in "moo" plus "oink"—to pay homage to the two meats they contain. They can be served as part of an Italian-themed meal or as an appetizer. Try them on spiralized onions, zucchini, or other vegetable "noodles."

hickory
WOOD PELLETS

250°F (121°C)
GRILL TEMP

1 to 1½ hrs
COOK TIME

Serves **6** • Prep time **30 mins** • Rest time **5 mins**

1lb (450g) ground beef (85/15), well chilled

½lb (225g) Italian sausage, well chilled

1 large egg, beaten

½ cup finely grated Parmesan, Asiago, or Romano cheese

½ cup panko or other breadcrumbs

1 tsp Italian seasoning

1 tsp coarse salt

½ tsp freshly ground black pepper

1lb (450g) thin-sliced bacon, halved crosswise

low-carb barbecue sauce, (optional)

1. Preheat the grill to 250°F (121°C).

2. Place the ground beef, Italian sausage, egg, cheese, breadcrumbs, Italian seasoning, and salt and pepper in a large bowl. Wet your hands with cold water. Form your hands into claw shapes and combine the ingredients using a light touch.

3. Form the mixture into 24 equal-sized balls. Wrap each with a half strip of bacon and secure the ends with a toothpick.

4. Place the meatballs on the grate and smoke until the bacon has rendered its fat and the internal temperature reaches 160°F (71°C), about 1 to 1½ hours. Brush the meatballs with barbecue sauce (if using) during the last 10 minutes of smoking.

5. Transfer the meatballs to a platter. Let rest for 5 minutes before serving.

TIPS | *To preserve their round shape, thread the meatballs on bamboo skewers (4 meatballs per skewer), running the pointed tip through the bacon to secure it to the meatball. Place four firebricks upright on the grate facing each other, two per side. Balance the ends of the skewers between the bricks, suspending the meatballs above the grate. Instead of barbecue sauce, drizzle the meatballs with warmed Italian-style tomato sauce or marinara.*

Nutrition per 3 meatballs

Calories **489** • Total fat **41g** • Carbs **3g** • Dietary fiber **0g** • Sugars **1g** • Protein **27g**

Reverse-Seared Elk Tenderloin
with Green Peppercorn Sauce

hickory or oak
WOOD PELLETS

**225°F (107°C);
500°F (260°C)**
GRILL TEMP

64 to 66 mins
COOK TIME

Said to be invented by competition barbecuer Christopher Finney in 2001, reverse searing has captured the attention of pros and backyard barbecuers alike. Essentially, you indirectly cook meat to a temperature 10 to 15°F below your target and then sear over high heat to finish.

Serves **8** • Prep time **25 mins** • Rest time **10 mins**

1 whole elk tenderloin, about 2½lb (1.2kg)

extra virgin olive oil

coarse salt

fresh coarsely ground black pepper

granulated garlic

for the sauce

3 tbsp unsalted butter, divided

2 large shallots, peeled and finely diced

2 cups low-salt beef stock

½ cup Cognac or brandy

1 cup heavy whipping cream

1 tbsp Dijon mustard

¼ brined green peppercorns, drained

2 tbsp fresh coarsely ground dried green peppercorns

coarse salt

freshly ground black pepper

1. Preheat the grill to 225°F (107°C).

2. Tie the tenderloin at 2-inch (5cm) intervals with butcher's twine. Tuck the tail under the thicker portion of the tenderloin and secure with twine. Trim any loose strings close to the knots. Place the tenderloin on a rimmed sheet pan and use your hands to coat all the sides with olive oil. Generously season with salt and pepper and granulated garlic.

3. In a skillet on the stovetop over medium heat, make the sauce by melting 2 tablespoons of butter. Add the shallots and cook until softened but not browned, about 2 to 3 minutes. Add the beef stock and raise the heat to medium high. Bring the mixture to a boil and reduce to ½ cup, about 10 minutes. Add the Cognac and cream and then whisk in the mustard.

4. Crush some of the brined peppercorns with the side of a knife. Stir all the brined and dried peppercorns into the sauce. Cook until the sauce is thick enough to coat a spoon, about 3 minutes. Whisk in the remaining 1 tablespoon of butter. Season with salt and pepper to taste. Keep warm.

5. Place the tenderloin on the grate at an angle to the bars. Smoke until the internal temperature in the thickest part of the meat reaches 110 to 115°F (43 to 46°C), about 1 hour. Transfer the tenderloin to a rimmed sheet pan lined with aluminum foil.

6. Raise the temperature to 500°F (260°C). Place the tenderloin on the grate at an angle to the bars. Sear until the internal temperature reaches 135°F (57°C), about 2 to 3 minutes per side.

7. Transfer the meat to a cutting board. Remove the butcher's twine and slice the tenderloin into steaks. Place the slices on a platter. Rewarm and rewhisk the sauce if necessary. Spoon over the steaks before serving.

Nutrition per 6oz (170g)
Calories **344** • Total fat **20g** • Carbs **2g** • Dietary fiber **0g** • Sugars **0g** • Protein **33g**

Buffalo-Style Bison Burgers
with Celery Pickles

hickory or oak
WOOD PELLETS

**180°F (82°C);
450°F (232°C)**
GRILL TEMP

40 mins
COOK TIME

If you've never eaten bison, the meat is actually beefy-tasting. Because American bison are sometimes (wrongly) called buffalo, I took advantage of the play on words to recreate the iconic flavors that made the Anchor Bar in Buffalo, New York, famous. If you can't find ground bison, ground beef will work.

Serves **6** • Prep time **20 mins** • Rest time **none**

1½lb (680g) ground bison
coarse salt
freshly ground black pepper
4oz (110g) blue cheese crumbles

for the pickles
1 bunch of celery
2 garlic cloves, peeled and smashed with a chef's knife
2 tsp dried dill weed
2 tsp yellow mustard seeds
1½ tsp black peppercorns
½ tsp crushed red pepper flakes
1½ cups distilled water
½ cup distilled white vinegar
¼ cup coarse salt

for the glaze
4 tbsp unsalted butter
4 tbsp hot sauce

for serving
hamburger or brioche buns
lettuce leaves
thinly sliced red onions
reduced-fat mayo

1. Preheat the grill to 180°F (82°C).

2. Make the pickles by placing the celery stalks parallel to you on a cutting board. Trim several inches off the top, just below the leafy ends. Thinly cut the stalks at a sharp diagonal into ¼-inch (.5cm) pieces. Transfer to a bowl of cold water, rinse to dislodge any dirt, and then drain. Transfer the celery to a quart-size canning jar, leaving plenty of headroom. Add the remaining ingredients except the water, vinegar, and salt to the jar.

3. In a saucepan on the stovetop over medium-high heat, bring the water, vinegar, and salt to a boil. Stir until the salt dissolves. Pour the mixture over the celery. Set aside uncovered until cool and preferably up to 2 hours. (Cover and refrigerate for up to 1 week if not using immediately.)

4. In a small saucepan on the stovetop over low heat, make the glaze by melting the butter and stirring in the hot sauce. Keep warm.

5. Wet your hands with cold water and form the bison into 6 patties of equal size, each about ¾ inch (2cm) thick. Use your thumbs to make a shallow depression in the top of each burger. Season with salt and pepper.

6. Place the burgers on the grate and smoke for 30 minutes. Transfer the burgers to a plate and then raise the temperature to 450°F (232°C). Return the burgers to the grate and grill for 4 to 5 minutes and then turn. Brush the glaze on the seared side. Continue to cook until the internal temperature reaches 155°F (68°C), about 3 to 4 minutes more and then turn again. Brush the other side with the glaze.

7. Remove the burgers from the grill and top each with blue cheese crumbles. Place the burgers on buns or in lettuce. Top with red onions and mayo or your favorite condiments. Serve with the celery pickles.

Nutrition per 1 burger (without bun)
Calories **522** • Total fat **37g** • Carbs **7g** • Dietary fiber **2g** • Sugars **2g** • Protein **41g**

Venison Carne Asada

Carne asada literally means grilled or barbecued meat and doesn't refer to any particular cut. If you don't come from a family of hunters, feel free to substitute beef flank steak, skirt steak, hanger steak, or even thin boneless pork chops for the venison.

mesquite or oak
WOOD PELLETS

450°F (232°C)
GRILL TEMP

6 to 8 mins
COOK TIME

Serves **4** • Prep time **15 mins** • Rest time **3 mins**

1½lb (680g) venison steak, such as sirloin, about ¾ inch (2cm) thick

southwestern-style rub

12 large scallions or spring onions, cleaned and trimmed

for the marinade

2 garlic cloves, peeled and smashed with a chef's knife

1 jalapeño or serrano pepper, destemmed and thinly sliced

juice of 1 orange

juice of 1 lime

1 tbsp distilled white vinegar

1 tsp ground cumin

1 tsp coarse salt

⅓ cup vegetable oil

¼ cup chopped fresh cilantro

for serving

warmed flour or corn tortillas (optional)

lime wedges

sprigs of fresh cilantro

Salsa de Molcajete (page 26) or another salsa

1. In a small bowl, make the marinade by combining the garlic, jalapeño, orange juice, lime juice, white vinegar, cumin, and salt. Whisk until the salt dissolves. Whisk in the vegetable oil and stir in the cilantro. Place the venison in a resealable plastic bag and add the marinade, massaging the bag to thoroughly coat the meat. Refrigerate for 2 to 4 hours.

2. Preheat the grill to 450°F (232°C).

3. Drain the venison and remove any solids. (Discard the marinade.) Pat dry with paper towels. Lightly dust on both sides with the rub. Place the venison and scallions on the grate and sear until the internal temperature reaches 135°F (57°C), about 3 to 4 minutes per side. Grill the scallions until the bulbs are browned and tender, about 4 to 6 minutes, turning as needed.

4. Remove the meat and scallions from the grill. Place the venison on a cutting board and let rest for 3 minutes. Slice thinly on a sharp diagonal. Shingle the meat on a platter. Scatter the scallions and cilantro over the top. Serve with tortillas (if using), lime wedges, cilantro, and salsa.

TIPS | *While I wouldn't suggest using prized venison tenderloin or backstrap for this dish, other steak cuts are fair game. You want a cut that resembles beef flank steak or skirt steak. Feel free to butterfly a thicker piece of meat or even pound it with a meat tenderizer between sheets of plastic wrap to achieve the thickness you want.*

Nutrition per 6oz (170g)

Calories **268** • Total fat **8g** • Carbs **7g** • Dietary fiber **2g** • Sugars **3g** • Protein **39g**

Tuscan Cheesesteaks

Always a luxurious cut of meat, beef tenderloin becomes a real show-stopper when its been butterflied and stuffed with such quintessentially Italian ingredients as pesto, sun-dried tomatoes, provolone, and Parmigiano Reggiano. It could be the centerpiece of your holiday table.

olive or hickory
WOOD PELLETS

450°F (232°C)
GRILL TEMP

16 to 20 mins
COOK TIME

Serves **8 to 10** • Prep time **25 mins** • Rest time **3 mins**

2 tbsp extra virgin olive oil, plus more

12oz (340g) mixed wild or cremini mushrooms, cleaned and chopped

1 red bell pepper, trimmed, deseeded, and cut into ¼-inch (.5cm) strips

1 green bell pepper, trimmed, deseeded, and cut into ¼-inch (.5cm) strips

1 white onion, peeled and diced

3 garlic cloves, peeled and minced

1 center-cut beef tenderloin, about 4lb (1.8kg), trimmed

coarse salt

freshly ground black pepper

½ cup pesto, plus more

1 cup grated or shaved Parmigiano-Reggiano cheese

12 sun-dried tomatoes packed in olive oil, roughly chopped

12oz (340g) thinly sliced provolone cheese, preferably aged

1. Preheat the grill to 450°F (232°C).

2. In a large skillet on the stovetop over medium heat, warm the olive oil. Add the mushrooms and sauté until tender, about 8 minutes, stirring as needed. Transfer the mushrooms to a bowl.

3. Add the bell peppers, onion, and garlic to the skillet and cook until softened, about 5 to 6 minutes. Stir the mushrooms into the vegetable mixture. Remove the skillet from the heat and let the vegetables cool.

4. Place the tenderloin on a rimmed sheet pan. Make a lengthwise cut from one end to the other, but don't cut all the way through. (This is called "butterflying.") Open like a book and season the inside with salt and pepper. Spread the pesto on the inside of the meat with a small rubber spatula. Sprinkle the Parmigiano-Reggiano over the sauce. Place the tomatoes in a line in the center. Top with the vegetable mixture and provolone.

5. Cut five 12-inch (30.5cm) lengths of butcher's twine and place them at evenly spaced intervals under and perpendicular to the tenderloin. Bring the meat up over the stuffing and tie the pieces of twine together, snipping any loose ends. Coat the outside of the tenderloin with olive oil and season with salt and pepper.

6. Place the tenderloin on the grate at an angle to the bars. Grill until the cheese oozes out and the internal temperature reaches 125 to 130°F (52 to 54°C), about 4 to 5 minutes per side, turning with tongs.

7. Transfer the tenderloin to a cutting board and let rest for 3 minutes. Slice the tenderloin into 1-inch-thick (2.5cm) slices before serving.

TIP | *An electric or serrated knife works best for slicing the finished tenderloin.*

Nutrition per 7oz (200g)
Calories **669** • Total fat **39g** • Carbs **8g** • Dietary fiber **2g** • Sugars **2g** • Protein **68g**

New York Strip Steaks
with Blue Cheese Butter

hickory or pecan
WOOD PELLETS

450°F (232°C)
GRILL TEMP

6 to 8 mins
COOK TIME

Cut from the short loin, strip steak is tender and beefy-tasting. (You'll recognize it as the larger steak of the two that make up a porterhouse or T-bone; the smaller steak is the tenderloin.) Its natural umami flavors are amplified by the blue cheese butter. You can also use this recipe with ribeye steak.

Serves **4** • Prep time **15 mins** • Rest time **3 mins**

4 boneless New York strip steaks, each about 12oz (340g) and 1 inch (2.5cm) thick

coarse salt

freshly ground black pepper

for the butter

8 tbsp unsalted butter, at room temperature

1 garlic clove, peeled and finely minced

⅓ cup crumbled blue cheese, mashed with a fork

1 tbsp minced chives

1 tsp Worcestershire sauce

½ tsp fresh coarsely ground black pepper

1. Approximately 45 minutes before you're ready to cook, lightly season the steaks on both sides with salt and pepper. Place the steaks on a wire rack on a rimmed sheet pan.

2. Preheat the grill to 450°F (232°C).

3. In a small bowl, make the blue cheese butter by combining the ingredients. Mix thoroughly. Set aside.

4. Place the steaks on the grate at an angle to the bars. Sear until the internal temperature reaches 130°F (54°C), about 3 to 4 minutes per side, turning once.

5. Transfer the steaks to a platter and immediately top with a spoonful of room temperature blue cheese butter. Tent the steaks with aluminum foil for 2 to 3 minutes to encourage the butter to melt before serving.

TIPS | *If the thickness of your steaks exceeds 1 inch (2.5cm), you'd be better off following the reverse-sear method described on page 59. Use any leftover blue cheese butter on roasted vegetables or grilled bread.*

Nutrition per 1 steak
Calories **700** • Total fat **40g** • Carbs **1g** • Dietary fiber **0g** • Sugars **0g** • Protein **80g**

Santa Maria Tri-Tip
with Pico de Gallo

oak
WOOD PELLETS

180°F (82°C),
450°F (232°C)
GRILL TEMP

51 to 68 mins
COOK TIME

The rural California community of Santa Maria is the birthplace of the tri-tip, a cut from the bottom of the sirloin that until 1952 was typically ground into hamburger. Well marbled and richly flavored, tri-tip is sometimes described as a cross between brisket and steak.

Serves **4** • Prep time **5 mins** • Rest time **none**

1 tri-tip roast, about 2 to 2½lb (1 to 1.2kg)

coarse salt

freshly ground black pepper

granulated garlic or garlic powder

for the pico de gallo
8 Roma tomatoes, decored, deseeded, and diced

1 white onion, peeled and diced

1 serrano pepper, destemmed, deseeded, and minced, plus more

1 garlic clove, peeled and minced

juice of 1 lime

⅓ cup loosely packed cilantro leaves, chopped

1 tsp coarse salt

1. In a medium bowl, make the pico de gallo by combining the tomatoes, onion, serrano, garlic, lime juice, and cilantro. Stir gently with a rubber spatula and season with salt to taste. Cover and refrigerate for 2 hours.

2. Approximately 45 minutes before you're ready to cook, season the roast on all sides with salt and pepper and granulated garlic.

3. Preheat the grill to 180°F (82°C).

4. Place the roast on the grate and smoke until the internal temperature in the thickest part of the roast reaches 115°F (46°C), about 45 minutes to 1 hour. Transfer the roast to a plate.

5. Raise the temperature to 450°F (232°C). Place the roast on the grate and sear until the internal temperature in the thickest part of the roast reaches 130 to 135°F (54 to 57°C), about 3 to 4 minutes per side. For best results, don't cook beyond medium rare. (The thinner tail should satisfy any diner who prefers beef to be more well done.)

6. Remove the roast from the grill and thinly slice on a sharp diagonal against the grain. Serve with the pico de gallo.

TIPS | *In Central California, tri-tip is traditionally served with a green salad, garlic toast, and pinquito beans—small pink beans that are native to California and available online. Instead of pico de gallo, feel free to serve the tri-tip with the **Horseradish Sauce** on page 25.*

Nutrition per 6oz (170g)
Calories **497** • Total fat **25g** • Carbs **14g** • Dietary fiber **4g** • Sugars **8g** • Protein **25g**

Bistecca alla Fiorentina
with Mushroom Ragout

Bistecca alla Fiorentina—Florentine steak—is a specialty of Florence. Sourced from the Chianina breed of cattle, it starts with an enormous porterhouse: on one side of the T-shaped bone is a strip steak and on the other is a tenderloin. Grilled over a wood fire, it's always served rare.

olive or oak
WOOD PELLETS

450°F (232°C)
GRILL TEMP

20 to 25 mins
COOK TIME

Serves **3 to 4** • Prep time **20 mins** • Rest time **5 mins**

2 sprigs of fresh sage

2 sprigs of fresh rosemary

2 sprigs of fresh thyme

1 porterhouse steak, about 2½lb (1.25kg)

extra virgin olive oil

coarse salt

fresh coarsely ground black pepper

for the ragout

3 tbsp unsalted butter

3 shallots or 1 white onion, peeled and chopped

2 garlic cloves, peeled and minced

2lb (1kg) wild mushrooms, cleaned, destemmed, and sliced or chopped

coarse salt

freshly ground black pepper

2 tbsp Cognac or brandy

½ cup low-salt beef broth, plus more

2 tsp light soy sauce

2 tsp chopped fresh thyme or 1 tsp dried thyme

½ cup heavy whipping cream, plus more

freshly squeezed lemon juice

freshly chopped chives

1. Place a cast iron skillet or cast iron griddle on the grate. Preheat the grill to 450°F (232°C).

2. In a large skillet on the stovetop over medium heat, begin making the ragout by melting the butter. Add the shallots and sauté until they soften, about 2 to 3 minutes, stirring often. Add the garlic and mushrooms. Season with salt and pepper. Cook until the mushrooms give up their liquid and begin to brown, about 5 minutes. Add the Cognac and cook for 1 minute. Stir in the broth, soy sauce, and thyme. Cook until the liquid reduces slightly, about 5 minutes. Remove the skillet from the stovetop and set aside.

3. Tie the sprigs of sage, rosemary, and thyme together with butcher's twine. Place the steak on a rimmed sheet pan and use the herb brush to generously brush both sides with olive oil. Season with salt and pepper.

4. Place the steak on the skillet and grill until the internal temperature reaches 125°F (52°C), about 8 to 10 minutes per side, occasionally using the herb brush to brush the steak with olive oil. If your grill has enough clearance, stand the porterhouse upright, resting on the bone, and continue to cook for a few minutes more.

5. Transfer the meat to a cutting board and brush it one final time with olive oil. Let rest for 5 minutes.

6. Add the cream to the ragout and reheat over medium-high heat until the mixture boils. Taste for seasoning, adding salt and pepper. If the ragout seems dry, add more cream or broth. If the flavors need brightening, stir in 1 or 2 teaspoons of lemon juice. Transfer the ragout to an attractive serving bowl and top with chives.

7. Carve off the strip steak and filet mignon. Slice them on a diagonal, keeping the slices in order. Place the bone on a platter and then place the slices around the bone. Serve immediately with the mushroom ragout.

Nutrition per 8oz (225g)

Calories **789** • Total fat **38g** • Carbs **10g** • Dietary fiber **0g** • Sugars **1g** • Protein **93g**

Beef Chuck Ribs

Beef chuck short ribs—not to be confused with plate ribs—require several hours on the grill at low and slow temperatures but will reward the patient pitmaster with rich, unctuous meat. Serve with roasted vegetables or shred for some of the most satisfying tacos of your life.

hickory, oak, or mesquite
WOOD PELLETS

250°F (121°C)
GRILL TEMP

4 to 5 hours
COOK TIME

Serves **4** • Prep time **5 mins** • Rest time **3 mins**

½ cup yellow or Dijon mustard

2 tbsp Worcestershire sauce

8 bone-in beef chuck ribs, about 2 to 2½lb (1 to 1.2kg) total

coarse salt

fresh coarsely ground black pepper

steak sauce or **Horseradish Sauce** (page 25)

for the mop sauce

1 cup low-carb beer or sugar-free dark-colored soda

½ cup cold brewed coffee

2 tbsp light soy sauce or liquid aminos

2 tbsp unsalted butter, melted

1. Preheat the grill to 250°F (121°C).

2. In a food-safe spray bottle, make the mop sauce by combining the ingredients. Set aside.

3. In a small bowl, combine the mustard and Worcestershire sauce. Lightly brush the mixture on the meaty sides of the short ribs. Season with salt and pepper.

4. Place the ribs bone side down on the grate and smoke until the internal temperature reaches 200°F (93°C), about 4 to 5 hours. Occasionally spritz the meat with the mop sauce after the first hour—about every 30 minutes.

5. Transfer the short ribs to a platter. Serve with steak sauce.

TIPS | *Sometimes called English short ribs, chuck ribs typically come in 3- to 4-inch lengths (7.5 to 10cm), often four to a package. Be sure to buy them with the bone attached because it helps the meat hold its shape during the long smoke.*

Nutrition per 2 short ribs

Calories **701** • Total fat **53g** • Carbs **4g** • Dietary fiber **1g** • Sugars **2g** • Protein **46g**

Spiced Lamb Burgers
with Tzatziki

oak
WOOD PELLETS

450°F (232°C)
GRILL TEMP

10 mins
COOK TIME

Once combined, the lamb mixture is quite versatile. You can form it into sliders, meatloaf, meatballs (I like to stuff them with goat cheese), or the kebabs known as *kofta* in the Middle East. Instead of serving individual accompaniments, you can also put together a large Greek salad.

Serves **4** • Prep time **15 mins** • Rest time **2 mins**

1½lb (680g) ground lamb or a mixture of lamb and beef, well chilled

⅓ cup grated red onion

1 to 2 garlic cloves, peeled and minced

2 tbsp chopped fresh dill or fresh mint

1 tsp ground cumin

½ tsp ground cinnamon

½ tsp crushed red pepper flakes (optional)

extra virgin olive oil

coarse salt

freshly ground black pepper

for the tzatziki

⅓ hothouse cucumber, unpeeled and coarsely grated

coarse salt

1½ cups plain Greek yogurt, drained

1 to 2 garlic cloves, peeled

1 tbsp freshly squeezed lemon juice or white distilled vinegar

1½ tbsp extra virgin olive oil

1 tbsp chopped fresh dill or fresh mint

1. Preheat the grill to 450°F (232°C).

2. Make the tzatziki by placing the cucumber in a sieve and lightly sprinkle with salt. After 15 minutes, rinse with cold running water. Drain and then squeeze the cucumber dry with paper towels. Transfer the cucumber to a large bowl. Add the yogurt, garlic, and lemon juice. Stir to mix. Season with salt to taste. Transfer to a serving bowl. Set aside. Just before serving, drizzle with the olive oil and scatter the fresh dill over the top.

3. In a large bowl, combine the lamb, red onion, garlic, dill, cumin, cinnamon, and red pepper flakes (if using). Wet your hands with cold water and mix thoroughly but gently. (Try not to overhandle the meat.) Form the meat into 4 patties of equal size, each about ¾ inch (2cm) thick. Use your thumbs to make a shallow depression in the top of each burger. Lightly oil the outsides of the burgers with olive oil. Season with salt and pepper.

4. Place the burgers on the grate and grill until the internal temperature reaches 160°F (71°C), about 4 to 5 minutes per side, turning once.

5. Transfer the burgers to a platter. On a separate platter, place thinly sliced red onions, thinly sliced tomatoes, thinly sliced cucumbers, crumbled feta, and Kalamata olives. Serve with the tzatziki and pita bread.

TIPS | *Salting and draining the cucumbers to extract excess moisture is a process called "degorging." This method is often used with eggplant. Instead of making burgers, feel free to form the meat mixture into meatballs.*

Nutrition per 1 burger
Calories **604** • Total fat **48g** • Carbs **6g** • Dietary fiber **1g** • Sugars **4g** • Protein **38g**

Triple Threat Pork Fatty
with Stuffed Jalapeños

Essentially meatloaf enrobed in bacon, the pork fatty made its debut on the barbecue scene several years ago and shows no sign of waning in popularity. While it's not exactly diet food, it *is* low in carbs. And too good not to eat at least once in your life. (Try it for breakfast!)

hickory
WOOD PELLETS

275°F (135°C)
GRILL TEMP

2 to 2½ hours
COOK TIME

Serves **10** • Prep time **30 mins** • Rest time **10 mins**

16 strips of bacon, about 1¼lb (565g) total, not thick cut

1½ tsp Tajin seasoning, plus more

8oz (225g) light cream cheese, at room temperature

3 large jalapeños, decored, destemmed, and deseeded

1lb (450g) seasoned breakfast sausage

1lb (450g) ground pork

6 to 8oz (170 to 225g) thinly sliced pepper Jack cheese

1. Preheat the grill to 275°F (135°C).

2. Moisten a workspace with a damp towel. Place a 15-inch (38cm) rectangle of plastic wrap on the workspace. Place 8 strips of bacon, sides touching, parallel to the edge of the plastic. Fold back the even-numbered strips at the halfway point and place a 9th snugly against the folds (perpendicular to the first 8). Unfold.

3. Fold back the odd-numbered strips and place a 10th snugly against the folds. Unfold. Repeat until the weave is complete. Place another sheet of plastic over the weave. Use a rolling pin to thin and tighten the weave.

4. In a small bowl, combine the Tajin and cream cheese. Tightly stuff each jalapeño with the mixture. Reserve any extra filling.

5. Place the sausage and pork in a large bowl. Wet your hands with cold water and knead the meats to combine. Transfer to a resealable plastic bag. Use a rolling pin to create a rectangle that's smaller than the dimensions of your bacon weave. (For reference, place the weave alongside the bag.) Slit the sides of the bag to release the meat and then position the bag over the weave and remove the remaining plastic.

6. Cover the meat with the pepper Jack, leaving 1 inch (2.5cm) around the edges. Pipe the reserved cream cheese mixture randomly over the surface. Position the stuffed jalapeños end to end on the long side of the meat. Use the plastic under the weave to tightly roll up the fatty from the side with the jalapeños. Use bamboo skewers to secure the weave. Lightly season the outside with more Tajin seasoning.

7. Place the fatty seam side down on the grate and smoke until the internal temperature reaches 160°F (71°C), about 2 to 2½ hours.

8. Transfer the fatty to a cutting board and let rest for 10 minutes. Use an electric knife to slice the fatty into 1-inch (2.5cm) rounds before serving.

Nutrition per 1 slice

Calories **832** • Total fat **75g** • Carbs **3g** • Dietary fiber **0g** • Sugars **0g** • Protein **35g**

Pork Loin Porchetta

According to culinary historians, Italians were enjoying this herb-scented roulade of pork as early as the 13th century. This version, featuring pork loin instead of a deboned pig, is much simplified but still offers a heady mix of fresh herbs, garlic, and lemon zest.

Serves **8 to 10** • Prep time **25 mins** • Rest time **10 mins**

oak
WOOD PELLETS

**450°F (232°C);
325°F (163°C)**
GRILL TEMP

1½ to 2 hrs
COOK TIME

1 center-cut pork loin roast, about 2½ to 3lb (1.2 to 1.4kg)

Mustard Caviar (page 26)

for the paste

4 garlic cloves, peeled and coarsely chopped

zest and juice of 1 lemon

½ cup coarsely chopped fresh curly or flat-leaf parsley

2 tbsp coarsely chopped fresh rosemary

2 tbsp coarsely chopped fresh sage

2 tsp fennel seeds

1 tsp coarse salt, plus more

1 tsp freshly ground black pepper, plus more

1 tsp crushed red pepper flakes

¼ cup extra virgin olive oil, plus more

1. Preheat the grill to 450°F (232°C).

2. Use a sharp, slender knife to slice the pork almost in half lengthwise, leaving a 1-inch (2.5cm) hinge. (This is called "butterflying.") Open like a book and make a similar lengthwise cut on either side of the first cut—stopping when you reach the last 1 inch (2.5cm) of meat.

3. In a food processor, make the seasoning paste by combining the garlic, lemon zest and juice, parsley, rosemary, sage, fennel seeds, salt and pepper, and red pepper flakes. With the machine running, add the olive oil in a thin stream. Thinly spread the paste on the interior surfaces of the pork loin, leaving a 1-inch (2.5cm) border. Starting on a long side, reform the pork loin and tie at 2-inch (5cm) intervals with butcher's twine. Brush the outside surface with olive oil and then season with salt and pepper.

4. Place the pork on the grate and roast for 30 minutes. Lower the temperature to 325°F (163°C) and continue to roast the pork until the internal temperature reaches 145°F (63°C), about 60 to 90 minutes more.

5. Transfer the porchetta to a cutting board and let rest for 10 minutes. Remove the butcher's twine and carve the meat into finger-thick slices. Serve with the mustard caviar or a good-quality aged balsamic vinegar.

TIPS | *You can also use the seasoned salt on page 48 to season the outside of the pork. Its flavors echo those of the seasoning paste. A serrated knife or a serrated electric knife works best for carving the roast.*

Nutrition per 6oz (170g)
Calories **380** • Total fat **28g** • Carbs **1g** • Dietary fiber **0g** • Sugars **0g** • Protein **31g**

Whiskey- & Cider-Brined Pork Shoulder

hickory
WOOD PELLETS

250°F (121°C)
GRILL TEMP

7 to 9 hrs
COOK TIME

Pork shoulder (often sold as pork butt or Boston butt) is one of the most forgiving barbecued meats there is. Although it can be sliced, most pitmasters prefer to barbecue it until the collagen and connective tissue break down sufficiently to "pull" it into meaty shreds.

Serves **8** • Prep time **20 mins** • Rest time **20 mins**

1 bone-in pork shoulder, about 5 to 7lb (2.3 to 3.2kg)

fresh coarsely ground black pepper

granulated garlic

1 cup apple juice or apple cider

low-carb barbecue sauce, warmed

hamburger buns (optional)

for the brine
1 gallon (3.8 liters) cold distilled water

1 cup coarse salt

1¼ cup whiskey, divided

⅓ cup light brown sugar or low-carb substitute

1. In a large saucepot on the stovetop over medium-high heat, make the brine by bringing the water, salt, 1 cup of whiskey, and brown sugar to a boil. Stir with a long-handled wooden spoon until the salt and sugar dissolve. Let the brine cool to room temperature. Cover and cool completely in the refrigerator.

2. Submerge the pork in the brine. If it floats, place a resealable bag of ice on top. Refrigerate for 24 hours.

3. Preheat the grill to 250°F (121°C).

4. Remove the pork shoulder from the brine and pat dry with paper towels. (Discard the brine.) Season the pork with pepper and granulated garlic. Place the pork on the grate and smoke until the internal temperature reaches 165°F (74°C), about 5 hours.

5. Transfer the pork to an aluminum foil roasting pan and add the apple juice and the remaining ¼ cup of whiskey. Cover tightly with aluminum foil. Place the pan on the grate and cook the pork until the bone releases easily from the meat and the internal temperature reaches 200°F (93°C), about 3 hours more. (Be careful when lifting a corner of the foil to check on the roast because steam will escape.)

6. Remove the pan from the grill and let the pork rest for 20 minutes. Reserve the juices.

7. Wearing heatproof gloves, pull the pork into chunks. Discard the bone or any large lumps of fat. Pull the meat into shreds and transfer to a clean aluminum foil roasting pan. Moisten with the barbecue sauce or serve the sauce on the side. Stir in some of the drippings—not too much because you don't want the pork to be swimming in its juices. Serve on buns (if using).

Nutrition per 4oz (110g)
Calories **733** • Total fat **54g** • Carbs **7g** • Dietary fiber **0g** • Sugars **6g** • Protein **45g**

Korean Pulled Pork Lettuce Wraps

Are you ready to take your pulled pork to the next level? Including *gochujang* (Korean chili paste) and *gochugaru* (Korean chili powder) to the sauce will help you retool this Carolinean specialty. Lettuce leaves (romaine or butter lettuce) stand in for carb-heavy buns.

oak
WOOD PELLETS

250°F (121°C)
GRILL TEMP

7 to 8 hrs
COOK TIME

Serves **8** • Prep time **10 mins** • Rest time **20 mins**

1 bone-in pork shoulder, about 6lb (2.7kg)

1 cup low-carb beer or sugar-free light-colored soda

for the sauce

1½ cups low-carb barbecue sauce

¼ cup low-carb beer or sugar-free light- or dark-colored soda

3 tbsp gochujang

3 tbsp light soy sauce

1 tbsp rice wine vinegar

1 tbsp toasted Asian sesame oil

1 tsp gochugaru

for the rub

3 tbsp coarse salt

3 tbsp gochugaru

3 tbsp granulated light brown sugar or low-carb substitute

2 tsp granulated garlic

2 tsp onion powder

1 tsp ground ginger

1. Preheat the grill to 250°F (121°C).

2. In a small bowl, make the barbecue sauce by whisking together the ingredients. Cover and refrigerate until ready to serve.

3. In a small bowl, make the rub by combining the ingredients. Rinse the meat with cold running water and pat dry with paper towels. Sprinkle the rub evenly over the surface, using your fingertips to pat it on.

4. Place the pork shoulder on the grate and smoke until the internal temperature reaches 165°F (74°C), about 4 to 5 hours. Transfer the meat to an aluminum foil roasting pan. Add the beer and then cover the pan tightly with heavy-duty aluminum foil. Continue to cook until the internal temperature reaches 200°F (93°C), about 3 hours more. (Keep the probe from touching bone or it will give you a false reading.) When the pork is tender enough to pull, the meat will release easily from the bone.

5. Transfer the pork shoulder to a cutting board. Drain the accumulated juices into a separate container and reserve. While the pork is still hot, pull out the bone and separate the meat into chunks. Using meat claws, forks, or your fingers, pull the meat into shreds, discarding any lumps of fat or undesirable bits. Return the meat to the pan. Stir in some of the reserved cooking juices if desired. You want the pork to be moist but not soupy.

6. Wrap the hot pork in lettuce leaves. Top with thinly sliced garlic, thinly sliced crosswise jalapeños, toasted sesame seeds, pickled ginger, and barbecue sauce. You can also serve the pork the American way: piled high on sesame seed buns.

Nutrition per 3oz (170g)

Calories **588** • Total fat **44g** • Carbs **11g** • Dietary fiber **1g** • Sugars **7g** • Protein **36g**

Baby Back Ribs
with Mustard Slather

You could also call these baby backs "ribs in a hurry" because you can put them on the table in about 2 hours versus the usual 5 to 6 they take when barbecued "low and slow." The ribs still come out tender and juicy and suffused with the flavors of spices and wood smoke.

hickory or apple
WOOD PELLETS

325°F (163°C)
GRILL TEMP

1½ to 2 hrs
COOK TIME

Serves **4** • Prep time **10 mins** • Rest time **5 mins**

2 racks of baby back ribs, each about 2lb (1kg)

all-purpose barbecue rub

low-carb barbecue sauce (optional)

for the mustard
½ cup yellow or brown mustard

2 tbsp dill pickle juice or apple cider vinegar

1. Preheat the grill to 325°F (163°C).

2. Remove the thick membrane on the bone side of the ribs. Don't remove the thin membrane on top of the bones because it holds them together. Trim off any odd bits of meat or excess fat. Place the ribs on a rimmed sheet pan.

3. In a small bowl, make the mustard slather by combining the mustard and pickle juice. Brush the ribs on both sides with the mixture and then season with the barbecue rub.

4. Place the ribs on the grate and smoke until the ribs are tender, about 1½ to 2 hours. (A toothpick inserted between bones should go in with little resistance. The meat will also have pulled back from the bone about ½ inch [1.25cm].) Brush the ribs with barbecue sauce (if using) during the last 10 minutes of smoking. Place the ribs meat side down on the grate for 5 minutes. Turn and grill for 5 minutes more. This sets the sauce.

5. Transfer the ribs to a cutting board. Use a sharp knife to cut the slabs in half or into individual ribs. Serve immediately with more barbecue sauce.

TIPS | *Use a table knife or butter knife to pry up the membrane on one of the middle bones. Grab the membrane with a paper towel and pull it off. You can easily double this recipe to feed a larger crowd. If your grill space is limited, you might want to invest in a rib rack. This device holds the ribs upright, substantially reducing the area they require. (See page 19.) Another trick is to coil the ribs and secure them with bamboo skewers.*

Nutrition per ¼ slab
Calories **720** • Total fat **61g** • Carbs **2g** • Dietary fiber **1g** • Sugars **0g** • Protein **42g**

Pork & Pepperoni Burgers

This is one of those dishes that's easily customizable: Fill the pork burger with your favorite pizza toppings, such as sautéed mushrooms, red or green peppers, onions, olives, or whatever you usually like on your pizza. Use the blueprint below to help you create your own version of pizza burgers.

hickory or pecan
WOOD PELLETS

300°F (149°C)
GRILL TEMP

50 mins to 1 hr
COOK TIME

Serves **4** • Prep time **20 mins** • Rest time **3 mins**

1lb (450g) bulk pork sausage, preferably Italian

1lb (450g) ground pork, well chilled

8 slices of bacon, preferably thick-cut

8oz (225g) grated mozzarella cheese, plus more

1 tsp Italian seasoning

½ cup pizza sauce

1½oz (40g) pepperoni, roughly chopped

1. Wet your hands with cold water. In a large bowl, combine the sausage and ground pork until well mixed. Line a rimmed sheet pan with aluminum foil. Divide the meat into 4 equal-sized balls and place on the sheet pan. Spray the lower third of a soda can (including the bottom) with cooking spray. Firmly press the can into one of the meatballs to create a meat bowl with uniform sides. Gently twist or rock the can to remove. Use your hands to repair any cracks in the bowl.

2. Wrap 2 slices of bacon around the circumference of the bowl and secure with toothpicks. Repeat with the remaining meatballs, respraying the can with cooking spray as necessary. Chill for 1 hour.

3. Preheat the grill to 300°F (149°C).

4. Place the patties cup side up on the grate and grill for 30 minutes. Use paper towels to blot any grease that pools at the bottom of the cups.

5. Sprinkle 2 tablespoons of cheese into each cup. Top each patty with equal amounts of Italian seasoning, pizza sauce, and pepperoni. Generously sprinkle more cheese over the top. Continue to grill until the bacon crisps, the cheese melts, and the internal temperature reaches 160°F (71°C), about 20 to 30 minutes more.

6. Remove the burgers from the grill and rest for 3 minutes. Remove the toothpicks and serve immediately.

TIPS | *Spraying the can with cooking spray (or oiling with vegetable oil) will prevent the can from sticking to the meat when you try to remove it. Don't skip this step. This hefty burger needs no bun. Serve it with a knife and fork.*

Nutrition 1 burger

Calories **941** • Total fat **73g** • Carbs **2g** • Dietary fiber **0g** • Sugars **1g** • Protein **65g**

Home-Cured Hickory-Smoked Bacon

One of the most satisfying barbecue projects you can try is making from-scratch hickory-smoked bacon. No smokehouse needed—just a pellet grill. Yes, it takes several days to make from start to finish—with little hands-on time—but the results are worth the patience.

hickory
WOOD PELLETS

200°F (93°C)
GRILL TEMP

2 to 3 hrs
COOK TIME

Makes **3½lb (1.6kg)** • Prep time **40 mins** • Rest time **none**

1 pork belly, about 5lb (2.3kg) and 1½ inches (3.75cm) thick, rind removed

for the cure
⅓ cup kosher salt

⅓ light brown sugar, turbinado sugar, or maple sugar or low-carb substitute

3 tbsp freshly ground black pepper

3 bay leaves, crumbled

2 tsp pink curing salt #1

2 tsp granulated garlic

1. Rinse the pork belly under cold running water and pat dry with paper towels. Place in a resealable plastic bag.

2. In a small bowl, make the cure by combining the ingredients, ensuring to especially distribute the pink curing salt. Sprinkle the rub as evenly as possible on the pork belly and use your hands to thoroughly distribute it. (You might want to wear disposable gloves.) Close the bag and refrigerate for 7 days, turning once a day and occasionally massaging the spices into the meat. Some liquid will appear in the bag and the pork belly will start firming up.

3. Rinse the pork under cold running water and pat dry with paper towels. Place the pork belly on a wire rack placed on a rimmed sheet pan. Refrigerate uncovered for 48 hours so it has an opportunity to develop a pellicle—a surface that's very amenable to receiving smoke.

4. Preheat the grill to 200°F (93°C).

5. Place the sheet pan on the grate and smoke the pork until the internal temperature reaches 150°F (66°C), about 2 to 3 hours.

6. Remove the pan from the grill and let the bacon cool. Cover and refrigerate until it's firmed up again. Slice while cold and either grill or fry the first slices of the batch. Wrap the bacon in plastic wrap. Refrigerate for up to 1 week or freeze for up to 3 months.

Nutrition per 3oz (85g)
Calories **192** • Total fat **11g** • Carbs **2g** • Dietary fiber **0g** • Sugars **1g** • Protein **19g**

St. Louis–Style Pork Steaks

hickory or oak
WOOD PELLETS

250°F (121°C)
GRILL TEMP

2 hrs
COOK TIME

One of the best-kept secrets of regional barbecue is the pork steaks popular in St. Louis. Cut from pork shoulder, these steaks are seasoned, grilled, and then braised in a sweetish sauce called Maull's until they're impossibly tender. You can substitute with your favorite low-carb sauce.

Serves **4** • Prep time **10 mins** • Rest time **none**

1 cup low-carb barbecue sauce

¼ cup low-carb beer or sugar-free dark-colored soda or sugar-free root beer

4 bone-in pork shoulder steaks, each about 1lb (450g) and at least 1 inch (2.5cm) thick

for the rub

1 tbsp coarse salt

1 tbsp freshly ground black pepper

1 tbsp granulated light brown sugar or low-carb substitute

1 tbsp sweet or smoked paprika

1 tsp granulated garlic or garlic powder

1 tsp celery salt

1. Preheat the grill to 250°F (121°C).

2. In a small bowl, combine the barbecue sauce and beer. Set aside.

3. In a small bowl, make the rub by combining the ingredients. Mix well. Season the steaks on both sides with some of the rub.

4. Place the steaks on the grate at an angle to the bars and smoke for 30 minutes. Transfer the steaks to an aluminum foil roasting pan. Pour the barbecue mixture over them. Use tongs to turn the steaks, making sure each is coated well with the sauce.

5. Tightly wrap aluminum foil over the top of the pan and place it on the grate. Braise the steaks until they're fork tender, about 1½ hours. (Protect your hands when lifting a corner of the foil because steam will escape.)

6. Remove the pan from the grill and serve the steaks immediately.

TIPS | *If the steaks have a collar of fat around the outside, vertically score the fat at intervals to prevent the steaks from curling as they cook. You can serve the steaks directly from the pan or you can move them to the grate for 30 minutes to set the sauce.*

Nutrition per ½ steak

Calories **543** • Total fat **43g** • Carbs **4g** • Dietary fiber **1g** • Sugars **3g** • Protein **35g**

Smoke-Roasted Beer-Braised Brats

They take their brats seriously in Sheboygan and other parts of Wisconsin. Although it's not traditional, I like to serve smoked sauerkraut with this meal. Simply transfer prepared sauerkraut to an aluminum foil roasting pan and smoke at 225°F (107°C) for 1 hour.

hickory
WOOD PELLETS

325°F (163°C)
GRILL TEMP

60 to 65 mins
COOK TIME

Serves **8** • Prep time **20 mins** • Rest time **none**

8 Wisconsin-style bratwursts

low-carb beer (enough to cover the brats)

2 tbsp unsalted butter

2 large sweet onions, peeled and sliced crosswise

2 garlic cloves, peeled and smashed with a chef's knife

8 brat buns (optional)

coarse ground mustard or German-style mustard

1. Preheat the grill to 325°F (163°C).

2. Place the brats on the grate at a diagonal to the bars. (Don't pierce the brats or the juices will run out.) Grill until the skin is nicely browned, about 40 to 45 minutes.

3. In a Dutch oven on the stovetop over medium-high heat, bring the beer, butter, onions, and garlic to a boil. Transfer the Dutch oven to the grill.

4. Use tongs to transfer the brats to the Dutch oven and let them steep for at least 20 minutes. The brats will stay at serving temperature—160°F (71°C)—for 1 hour or more.

5. Remove the Dutch oven from the grill and serve the brats on buns (if using) with mustard.

TIPS | *This is a great recipe for tailgating or other parties when the time to eat isn't set in stone. Insert the probe through the end of the sausage.*

Nutrition per 1 brat

Calories **365** • Total fat **30g** • Carbs **7g** • Dietary fiber **1g** • Sugars **2g** • Protein **11g**

Pork Tenderloin
with Bourbon Peaches

hickory
WOOD PELLETS

400°F (204°C)
GRILL TEMP

20 to 27 mins
COOK TIME

One of the most economical and low-fat choices at the meat counter, pork tenderloin goes phenomenally well with peaches stewed with a splash of bourbon. Seek out freestone peaches because they release their pits easily. Peaches not in season? Substitute diced apples.

Serves **6 to 8** • Prep time **15 mins** • Rest time **5 mins**

2 pork tenderloins, about 2lb (1kg) total, trimmed of silver skin and excess fat

extra virgin olive oil

for the rub

3 tbsp coarse salt

3 tbsp freshly ground black pepper

3 tbsp smoked or regular paprika

3 tbsp granulated light brown sugar or low-carb substitute

2 tbsp instant coffee

1 tbsp granulated garlic

2 tsp ground cumin

1 tsp chili powder

for the peaches

4 freestone peaches, about 1lb (450g) total, peeled, pitted, and sliced

1 tbsp freshly squeezed lemon juice

¼ cup unsalted butter

4 tbsp granulated light brown sugar or low-carb substitute

2 tbsp bourbon

½ tsp ground cinnamon

½ tsp pure vanilla extract

pinch of coarse salt

1. Place a cast iron skillet on the grate. Preheat the grill to 400°F (204°C).

2. In a small bowl, make the rub by combining the ingredients. Coat the tenderloins in olive oil and season with the rub.

3. Place the peaches and lemon juice in a medium bowl, turning the peaches gently to coat. Measure the other ingredients and then take them and the peaches grill side.

4. Place 1 tablespoon of olive oil in the hot skillet and add the tenderloins. Quickly sear the pork, about 2 to 3 minute per side, turning as needed with tongs. When they're nicely browned, transfer the tenderloins to the grate. Cook until the internal temperature in the thickest part of the meat reaches 145°F (63°C), about 8 minutes. For moist meat, don't cook the tenderloins beyond 155°F (68°C).

5. Transfer the pork to a cutting board and tent with aluminum foil.

6. Replace the cast iron skillet with a clean one and close the grill lid to let it heat. Once hot, make the bourbon peaches by melting the butter. Add the brown sugar, bourbon, cinnamon, vanilla, and salt. Cook the mixture until it bubbles, about 5 to 8 minutes. Add the peaches and cook for 5 to 8 minutes more, turning the peaches carefully with a spoon to coat. Carefully transfer the skillet to a trivet or another heatproof surface.

7. Slice the pork on a diagonal into ½-inch (1.25cm) slices. Shingle the slices on a platter. Spoon the peaches around the pork or serve separately.

Nutrition per 6oz (170g)
Calories **374** • Total fat **16g** • Carbs **23g** • Dietary fiber **1g** • Sugars **23g** • Protein **33g**

Spiced Pork Belly

If you've only ever eaten cured bacon, you'll be surprised at the myriad ways to serve uncured pork belly. Try it in tacos, ramen, salads, or mixed with roasted vegetables. The two-tiered cooking method is one inspired by Chef David Chang at his award-winning NYC restaurant Momofuku.

apple or another fruitwood
WOOD PELLETS

450°F (232°C); 275°F (135°C)
GRILL TEMP

98 to 130 mins
COOK TIME

Serves **4** • Prep time **10 mins** • Rest time **3 mins**

2lb (1kg) skinless pork belly

for the rub
2 tbsp fine kosher salt

2 tbsp granulated white or light brown sugar or low-carb substitute

2 tsp freshly ground black pepper

2 tsp ground mustard

2 tsp Chinese five-spice powder

1. In a small bowl, make the rub by combining the ingredients. Mix well. Lightly season the pork belly on all sides with the rub. Cover and refrigerate overnight.

2. Preheat the grill to 450°F (232°C).

3. Place the pork belly on the grate and roast for 30 minutes, turning once. Lower the temperature to 275°F (135°C). Roast the pork until tender and the internal temperature reaches 185°F (85°C), about 1 to 1½ hours more.

4. Remove the pork belly from the grill and let cool completely. Wrap tightly in plastic wrap and refrigerate until firm and well chilled.

5. Preheat the grill to 450°F (232°C).

6. Cut the pork belly into slices, slabs, or cubes. Place the pork on the grate and grill until the edges crisp, about 8 to 10 minutes, turning as needed.

7. Remove the pork from the grill and serve immediately.

TIPS | *Pork belly skin—also called the rind—has usually been removed. If not, use a sharp fillet knife to carefully separate the skin from the flesh. The skin can be cut into strips and used to make chicharrónes (fried pork skins). If you cut the pork into cubes instead, place them in an aluminum foil roasting pan and grill them until the edges crisp, about 6 to 8 minutes. Add the cubes to the **Pork Belly Salad** on page 151.*

Nutrition per 2oz (55g)
Calories **595** • Total fat **60g** • Carbs **3g** • Dietary fiber **0g** • Sugars **3g** • Protein **11g**

3-2-1 Spare Ribs

While some people like their ribs with a bit of chew, others prefer the meat to literally fall off the bone. The 3-2-1 formula plays to the latter group. You smoke the ribs for 3 hours, wrap them in foil for 2 hours, and then unwrap, sauce, and return them to the grill for the final hour.

hickory
WOOD PELLETS

225°F (107°C)
GRILL TEMP

6 hrs
COOK TIME

Serves **4**   •   Prep time **10 mins**   •   Rest time **5 mins**

2 racks of St. Louis–cut pork spare ribs, each about 3lb (1.4kg)

all-purpose barbecue rub

3 tbsp unsalted butter, cut into cubes

1 cup apple juice or apple cider

low-carb barbecue sauce

1. Preheat the grill to 225°F (107°C).

2. Place the ribs on a rimmed sheet pan and dust with the rub. Place the ribs bone side down on the grate and smoke for 3 hours.

3. Tear off 2 large sheets of heavy-duty aluminum foil. Place one rack of ribs bone side down on the foil and top with half the butter cubes. Place the second rack of ribs bone side down on the butter cubes and top with the remaining butter cubes.

4. Bring up all 4 sides of the foil and pour in the apple juice. Crimp the edges of the foil so the ribs are tightly enclosed. Place the foil package on the grate and smoke for 2 hours more.

5. Transfer the ribs to a workspace and carefully open the foil package. (Be careful of escaping steam.) Discard the foil and any accumulated juices. Brush the ribs on both sides with barbecue sauce. Place the ribs on the grate and smoke for 1 hour more to set the sauce and firm up the bark.

6. Transfer the ribs to a cutting board. Use a sharp knife to cut the slabs in half or into individual ribs. Serve immediately.

TIPS | *Don't overseason the ribs or they can become unpleasantly salty. During a long cook such as this one, the salt can even begin to cure them. For the same reason, don't apply the rub until you're ready to cook. If you find the ribs to be too tender using this method, modify it by smoking the ribs for only 2 hours rather than 3 hours.*

Nutrition per ¼ slab
Calories **680**   •   Total fat **45g**   •   Carbs **4g**   •   Dietary fiber **0g**   •   Sugars **4g**   •   Protein **63g**

Pig on a Stick
with Buffalo Glaze

One of the trendiest items on the menus of casual bars and restaurants is pig wings—succulent knobs of pork harvested from the back leg of a pig, just below the ham. If you glaze these diminutive pork shanks, be sure to use a milder Louisiana-style hot sauce.

hickory
WOOD PELLETS

180°F (82°C);
275°F (135°C);
325°F (163°C)
GRILL TEMP

5½ to 6½ hrs
COOK TIME

Serves **10 to 12** • Prep time **25 mins** • Rest time **none**

4lb (1.8kg) pork shanks, each about 4 to 6oz (110 to 170g), trimmed and thawed if frozen

1½ cups sugar-free dark-colored soda, sugar-free root beer, or no-sugar-added apple juice

for the brine (optional)
1 gallon (3.8 liters) distilled water
¾ cup kosher salt
5 tsp pink curing salt #1

for the glaze (optional)
½ cup unsalted butter
1 cup hot sauce
2 tsp granulated garlic
1 tsp Worcestershire sauce

1. In a stockpot on the stovetop over medium-high heat, make the brine by combining the ingredients and bringing the mixture to a boil. Stir until the salts dissolve. Remove the pot from the stovetop and let the brine cool to room temperature.

2. Add the pork shanks to the brine. Cover and refrigerate for 2 days.

3. Preheat the grill to 180°F (82°C).

4. Drain the pork shanks and discard the brine. (If you didn't brine the pork shanks, season them on all sides with your favorite barbecue rub.) Place the pork on the grate and smoke for 3 hours. Transfer the shanks to an aluminum roasting pan.

5. Raise the temperature to 275°F (135°C).

6. Add the soda to the pan and cover tightly with aluminum foil. Place the pan on the grate and braise the meat until it's tender but still attached to the bone, about 2 to 3 hours. Be careful when removing the foil because steam will escape. Remove the pan from the grill and set aside.

7. Raise the temperature to 325°F (163°C).

8. In a saucepan on the stovetop over medium heat, make the buffalo glaze by melting the butter. Stir in the remaining ingredients. Let the sauce simmer for 5 minutes to allow the flavors to blend.

9. Dip the pork shanks into the glaze and then transfer them to an aluminum foil roasting pan. Cover tightly with aluminum foil. Place the pan on the grate and cook the shanks until hot, about 30 minutes.

10. Remove the pan from the grill. Serve the pork with plenty of napkins.

Nutrition per 1 pork shank
Calories **445** • Total fat **34g** • Carbs **0g** • Dietary fiber **0g** • Sugars **0g** • Protein **32g**

First-Timer's Pulled Pork

hickory or apple
WOOD PELLETS

250°F (121°C)
GRILL TEMP

7 to 9 hrs
COOK TIME

New to smoking? Pulled pork is a great way to quickly boost your barbecue cred. Popular in western North Carolina, the tart and spicy sauce is a bit puckery on its own, but it's perfect when splashed on the smoke-infused pork. Your guests will never guess this is your first foray into pulled pork.

Serves **8 to 10** • Prep time **20 mins** • Rest time **1 hr**

1 bone-in pork shoulder, about 5 to 7lb (2.3 to 3.2kg)

coarse salt

freshly ground black pepper

1½ cups low-carb beer or sugar-free dark-colored soda

for the sauce

1½ cups apple cider vinegar

½ cup distilled water

2 tbsp ketchup

1½ tbsp granulated brown sugar or low-carb substitute

1 tsp coarse salt, plus more

1 tsp freshly ground black pepper

½ to 1 tsp crushed red pepper flakes

1. Preheat the grill to 250°F (121°C).

2. In a medium saucepan on the stovetop over medium-high, make the vinegar sauce by bringing the ingredients to a boil. Whisk to dissolve the sugar and salt. Let the sauce cool to room temperature and then transfer to a jar with a tight-fitting lid. Set aside.

3. Season the pork shoulder on all sides with salt and pepper. Place the pork on the grate and smoke until the bone releases easily from the meat and the internal temperature reaches 200°F (93°C), about 7 to 9 hours. Wrap the pork tightly in a large piece of heavy-duty aluminum foil and let rest in an insulated cooler for up to 1 hour.

4. Carefully remove the pork from the foil and reserve the juices. Wear heatproof gloves to pull the pork into chunks. Discard the bone and any large lumps of fat. Pull the meat into shreds and transfer to a clean aluminum foil roasting pan. Moisten with some of the reserved juices. Taste, adding more salt and pepper. Serve with the vinegar sauce.

TIPS | *Food-safe insulated rubber gloves are useful when pulling the pork—they'll help you grip the pork and protect your hands from the heat. (Pork must be pulled while it's still uncomfortably hot.) You can also pull the pork with your hands, two forks, or job-specific tools, such as meat claws.*

Nutrition per 4oz (110g)
Calories **614** • Total fat **41g** • Carbs **6g** • Dietary fiber **0g** • Sugars **5g** • Protein **48g**

Jamaican Jerk Pork Chops

Spicy, fiery, salty, and sweet, Jamaican jerk marinade is a natural complement to chicken. In this recipe, it gives pork a remarkable zing. The island's trademark Scotch bonnets can be difficult to find in the United States, so feel free to substitute the more widely available habanero.

hickory or oak
WOOD PELLETS

425°F (218°C)
GRILL TEMP

12 to 16 mins
COOK TIME

Serves **4** • Prep time **15 mins** • Rest time **2 mins**

4 thick pork rib or loin chops, each about 12oz (340g) and 1 inch (2.5cm) thick

for the marinade

½ to 1 Scotch bonnet or habanero pepper, destemmed, deseeded, and coarsely chopped, plus more

2 scallions, trimmed, white and green parts coarsely chopped

1 garlic clove, peeled and coarsely chopped

juice of 1 lime

2 tbsp vegetable oil

2 tbsp distilled water

1 tbsp light soy sauce

2 tsp coarsely chopped fresh thyme leaves

2 tsp peeled and minced fresh ginger

2 tsp dark brown sugar or low-carb substitute, plus more

1 tsp coarse salt, plus more

½ tsp freshly ground black pepper

½ tsp ground allspice

½ tsp ground nutmeg

½ tsp ground cinnamon

1. In a blender, make the jerk marinade by combining the ingredients. Blend until fairly smooth. Taste for seasoning, adding more Scotch bonnet, brown sugar, or salt. Place the pork chops in a resealable plastic bag and pour the marinade over them, turning and massaging the bag to thoroughly coat the meat. Refrigerate for 2 to 4 hours.

2. Preheat the grill to 425°F (218°C).

3. Remove the pork from the marinade and scrape off the excess. (Discard the marinade.) Grill the chops until the internal temperature reaches 145°F (63°C), about 6 to 8 minutes per side.

4. Transfer the chops to a platter. Let rest for 2 minutes before serving.

TIPS | *Scotch bonnets and habaneros are extremely hot peppers. Start with half a pepper (or less if you're heat-averse). Wear protective gloves when handling. To extract the most juice from limes, roll them on the countertop under a firm hand or microwave them on high for 15 seconds and then use a reamer.*

Nutrition per 1 chop

Calories **595** • Total fat **33g** • Carbs **6g** • Dietary fiber **0g** • Sugars **1g** • Protein **60g**

Home-Cured Picnic Ham
with Mustard Caviar

hickory or apple
WOOD PELLETS

**225°F (107°C);
325°F (163°C)**
GRILL TEMP

5½ to 7 hrs
COOK TIME

If you want to cure and smoke ham, a picnic ham is a good place to start. Although not technically a ham because it's from the foreleg (true hams come from the rear leg), they're still meaty. Also, don't be alarmed by the sugar and molasses. Little is absorbed by the meat.

Serves **8** • Prep time **30 mins** • Rest time **10 mins**

1 pork shoulder roast, about 5lb (2.3kg) total

1 cup distilled water, apple cider, or apple juice, plus more

Mustard Caviar (page 26)

for the brine

1 cup kosher salt

5 tsp pink curing salt #1

1 cup light brown sugar or turbinado sugar or low-carb substitute

¼ cup molasses or honey

1 gallon (3.8 liters) distilled water, divided, plus more

1. Trim any excess fat from the pork shoulder, leaving at least ¼ inch. Use a sharp knife to score the skin of the ham in the classic diamond pattern, making the cuts about 1 inch (2.5cm) apart, but don't penetrate the meat. (If you purchased a shoulder without skin, skip this step.)

2. In a stockpot on the stovetop over medium-high heat, make the brine by combining the salts, brown sugar, molasses, and water. Bring the mixture to a boil. Whisk to dissolve the salts and sugar. Remove the stockpot from the stovetop and let the brine cool to room temperature.

3. Submerge the pork shoulder in the brine. If it floats, place a resealable bag of ice on top. Refrigerate for 3 days.

4. Place the ham in a clean container and cover with cold water. Let the ham soak for 30 minutes. Drain and pat dry with paper towels.

5. Preheat the grill to 225°F (107°C).

6. Place the ham on the grate and grill until the internal temperature in the thickest part of the meat reaches 160°F (71°C), about 4 to 5 hours. Remove the ham from the grill. Let the ham come to room temperature. Cover and refrigerate for up to 3 days. This helps establish the ham's smokiness.

7. Preheat the grill to 325°F (163°C).

8. Transfer the ham to an aluminum foil roasting pan and add the water to the bottom of the pan. Place the pan on the grate and roast the ham until the skin is nicely browned and the internal temperature reaches 145°F (63°C), about 1½ to 2 hours.

9. Remove the ham from the grill and let rest for 10 minutes. Carve the ham and serve with the mustard caviar.

Nutrition per 3oz (85g)
Calories **427** • Total fat **27g** • Carbs **14g** • Dietary fiber **1g** • Sugars **12g** • Protein **35g**

POULTRY

Chicken Breast Calzones

Traditional calzones are usually a carb lover's delight: a heavy, bready meal. Here, the lean chicken breast itself becomes the pocket, holding sauce, melted cheese, fresh basil, and savory pepperoni. You won't miss the breading as you enjoy every flavorful morsel.

oak
WOOD PELLETS

425°F (218°C)
GRILL TEMP

20 to 24 mins
COOK TIME

Serves **4** • Prep time **20 mins** • Rest time **3 mins**

4 boneless, skinless chicken breasts, each about 6 to 8oz (170 to 225g)

coarse salt

freshly ground black pepper

1 cup good-quality Italian tomato sauce or marinara

4oz (110g) thinly sliced pepperoni or diced smoked ham

4oz (110g) provolone, fontina, or mozzarella cheese

8 fresh basil leaves

4 thin slices of prosciutto

extra virgin olive oil

freshly grated Parmesan cheese

1. Preheat the grill to 425°F (218°C).

2. Use a sharp, thin-bladed knife to cut a deep pocket in the side of each breast, angling the knife toward the opposite side. (Don't cut all the way through.) Season the inside of each breast with salt and pepper. Add a couple spoonfuls of tomato sauce to each pocket. Add 1 ounce (25g) of pepperoni, 1 ounce (25g) of provolone, and 2 basil leaves.

3. Wrap each breast crosswise with a slice of prosciutto and then pin each breast closed with two toothpicks. Lightly brush the breasts with olive oil and season the outside with salt and pepper.

4. Place the breasts on the grate at an angle to the bars. Grill for 10 to 12 minutes and then turn with a thin-bladed spatula. Dust the tops with grated Parmesan. Continue to cook until the chicken is cooked through and the cheese has melted, about 10 to 12 minutes more.

5. Transfer the chicken to a platter. Let rest for 3 minutes and then remove the toothpicks. Serve immediately.

TIPS | *The toothpicks will be easier to remove if you oil them before pinning the chicken breasts closed. Serve the calzones with a colorful green salad or on a bed of baby arugula dressed with extra virgin olive oil and lemon juice.*

Nutrition per 1 calzone

Calories **553** • Total fat **30** • Carbs **5g** • Dietary fiber **1g** • Sugars **2g** • Protein **65g**

Lemon & Herb Chicken

apple
WOOD PELLETS

400°F (204°C)
GRILL TEMP

1 hr 15 mins
COOK TIME

As written, this recipe suggests a dish perfect for springtime—maybe served with asparagus or baby greens. But it can also skew toward colder weather. Substitute a small orange for the lemon and sturdy herbs, such as rosemary, sage, and thyme, for the fragile ones.

Serves **3 to 4**   •   Prep time **15 mins**   •   Rest time **10 mins**

1 roaster chicken, about 4lb (1.8kg), preferably organic

1 large sweet onion, peeled and sliced lengthwise into 8 wedges

½ cup chicken stock or broth

sprigs of fresh rosemary, thyme, parsley, tarragon, or chives (or a mix)

lemon wedges

for the butter

4 tbsp unsalted butter, at room temperature

1 garlic clove, peeled and finely minced

2 tbsp chopped fresh herbs, such as rosemary, thyme, parsley, tarragon, or chives (or a mix)

2 tsp lemon zest

2 tsp freshly squeezed lemon juice

½ tsp coarse salt

½ tsp freshly ground black pepper

1. Preheat the grill to 400°F (204°C).

2. In a small bowl, make the herb butter by combining the ingredients.

3. Place the chicken on a rimmed sheet pan and tuck the lemon rinds from the butter into the main cavity. Rub the outside of the chicken with the herb butter. (Reserve any remainder.) Tuck the wings behind the back and tie the legs together with butcher's twine. Place the onion wedges in a shallow roasting pan to help form a natural rack for the chicken. (Alternatively, place several large carrots, trimmed and peeled, on the bottom of the pan.) Place the chicken on the onion rack. Add the chicken stock and any remaining herbed butter and lemon juice.

4. Place the roasting pan on the grate, roast the chicken for 30 minutes, and then baste with the juices from the bottom of the pan. Baste every 15 minutes until the chicken is golden brown and the internal temperature reaches 165°F (74°C), about 45 minutes more.

5. Transfer the chicken to a cutting board and let rest for 10 minutes. Carve the chicken and place the slices on a platter with a deep well. Spoon some of the juices over the chicken. Scatter fresh herbs over the top. Serve with the lemon wedges.

TIPS │ *Save the chicken carcass and the drippings for making stock or soup. A crisp Sauvignon Blanc would complement this dish nicely.*

Nutrition per ¼ chicken

Calories **1464**   •   Total fat **107g**   •   Carbs **6g**   •   Dietary fiber **1g**   •   Sugars **3g**   •   Protein **114g**

County Fair Turkey Legs

They first started making the rounds of Renaissance fairs in the 1980s and then migrated to some of the largest theme parks in the United States. I'm talking, of course, about gargantuan cured and smoked turkey legs. With a ham-like taste, they'll make you the hero of your tailgate party.

hickory
WOOD PELLETS

325°F (163°C)
GRILL TEMP

90 mins
COOK TIME

Makes **4** • Prep time **10 mins** • Rest time **5 mins**

4 turkey legs, each about 1lb (450g)

for the brine
½ gallon (1.9 liters) distilled water

½ cup kosher salt

¼ cup light brown sugar or low-carb substitute

2½ tsp pink curing salt #1

1 tsp liquid smoke (optional)

1. In a stockpot on the stovetop over medium-high heat, make the brine by combining the ingredients. Bring the mixture to a boil. Stir until the salts and sugar dissolve. Remove the pot from the stovetop and let the brine cool to room temperature. Cover and refrigerate until cool.

2. Submerge the turkey legs in the brine. If they float, place a resealable bag of ice on top. Refrigerate for 24 hours, turning from time to time so the legs cure evenly.

3. Preheat the grill to 325°F (163°C).

4. Remove the turkey legs from the brine and discard the liquid. Rinse the legs under cold running water and pat dry with paper towels.

5. Place the turkey legs on the grate and grill for 45 minutes. Turn and continue to cook until the turkey skin is nicely browned and the internal temperature in a leg reaches 170 to 175°F (77 to 79°C), about 45 minutes. (Turkey legs have a lot of connective tissue and they seem to turn out better when cooked to a slightly higher temperature.)

6. Remove the legs from the grill and serve warm or cold.

Nutrition per 1 turkey leg
Calories **657** • Total fat **31g** • Carbs **1g** • Dietary fiber **0g** • Sugars **1g** • Protein **89g**

Duck Breast
with Pomegranate Sauce

cherry
WOOD PELLETS

400°F (204°C)
GRILL TEMP

10 to 13 mins
COOK TIME

Thanks to a thick layer of fat, duck breast is one of the most challenging cuts of poultry to cook properly. By the time the skin is crisp and golden brown, the meat can be overcooked. The solution? Cooking the duck in a cast iron skillet you heat when you preheat the grill.

Serves **4** • Prep time **15 mins** • Rest time **5 mins**

4 duck breasts, each about 6oz (170g), skin on

for the rub
2 tsp coarse salt
1 tsp ground cumin
1 tsp ground coriander
1 tsp freshly ground black pepper
½ tsp ground cinnamon
½ tsp ground fennel

for the sauce
1 shallot, peeled and minced
1 cup pomegranate juice
1 tbsp sherry vinegar or balsamic vinegar
1 tsp cornstarch
¼ cup chicken stock or chicken broth
1 tbsp chilled unsalted butter, cut into 4 pieces
¼ cup fresh pomegranate seeds (optional)
1 tbsp minced fresh chives

1. Place a cast iron skillet on the grate. Preheat the grill to 400°F (204°C).

2. In a small bowl, make the rub by combining the ingredients. Use a sharp knife to diagonally score the skin of each duck breast—but don't nick the flesh. Lightly season the scored side of each breast.

3. Place the duck breasts skin side down in the skillet and sear until the skin is crisp and golden brown, about 8 to 10 minutes. Turn the breasts and cook until the internal temperature in the thickest part of a breast reaches 130°F (54°C), about 2 to 3 minutes more. Transfer the breasts to a plate.

4. In a large saucepan on the stovetop over medium heat, make the sauce by heating 1 tablespoon of duck fat from the skillet. (Reserve the remainder for another use.) Add the shallot and sauté until soft, about 2 to 3 minutes.

5. Add the pomegranate juice and bring the mixture to a boil over medium-high heat. Reduce the sauce by half, about 3 to 5 minutes. Add the vinegar and lower the heat to medium low.

6. Whisk together the cornstarch and chicken stock until smooth. Whisk into the sauce and cook until the sauce thickens, about 1 to 2 minutes. Whisk in the butter and stir in the pomegranate seeds (if using).

7. Place the duck breasts on a warm platter. Drizzle the pomegranate sauce over the top. Scatter the chives around the platter before serving.

TIPS | *A chef never discards the fat duck that breasts give off as they sear. Save it (you can freeze it) to sauté green beans, potatoes, etc.*

Nutrition per 1 breast
Calories **581** • Total fat **31g** • Carbs **9g** • Dietary fiber **0g** • Sugars **8g** • Protein **63g**

Jalapeño- & Cheese-Stuffed Chicken

Jalapeño and two kinds of cheese give these stuffed chicken pockets a delightful combination of flavors. You can eat these as an appetizer or as the main dish for a meal—great for a weekend party or for a weeknight dinner. Bacon and relatively high heat keep the chicken breasts moist as they cook.

mesquite
WOOD PELLETS

375°F (191°C)
GRILL TEMP

25 to 30 mins
COOK TIME

Serves **4** • Prep time **15 mins** • Rest time **2 mins**

4 boneless, skinless chicken breasts, each about 6 to 8oz (170 to 225g)

8 strips of thin-sliced bacon

for the filling

4oz (110g) light cream cheese, at room temperature

⅓ cup shredded pepper Jack or Cheddar cheese

2 jalapeños, destemmed, deseeded, and minced

2 tbsp reduced-fat mayo

1 tsp chili powder

½ tsp coarse salt

1. Preheat the grill to 375°F (191°C).

2. In a large bowl, make the filling by combining the ingredients. Mix well.

3. Use a sharp, thin-bladed knife to cut a deep pocket in the side of each chicken breast, angling the knife toward the opposite side. (Don't cut all the way through.) Spoon ¼ of the cheese filling into the pocket of each breast and gently press the edges of the pocket together to enclose. Wrap 2 slices of bacon in a spiral pattern around each breast.

4. Place the chicken on the grate at an angle to the bars. Grill until the chicken is cooked through, the filling melts, and the bacon is golden brown, about 25 to 30 minutes.

5. Transfer the pockets to a platter. Let rest for 2 minutes before serving.

TIPS | *The breasts can be filled up to 1 day ahead, covered with plastic wrap and refrigerated, and grilled just before serving. For extra juiciness, brine the chicken breasts for about 1 hour before slicing and stuffing. You'll need 1 quart (1 liter) of water and ¼ cup of coarse salt. Rinse under cold running water and dry before proceeding with the recipe.*

Nutrition per 1 pocket

Calories **447** • Total fat **28g** • Carbs **4g** • Dietary fiber **0g** • Sugars **0g** • Protein **43g**

Gen's Old-Fashioned Barbecued Chicken

hickory
WOOD PELLETS

350°F (177°C)
GRILL TEMP

75 to 90 mins
COOK TIME

My aunt Genevieve's barbecued chicken was the stuff of dreams. Working with a vintage grill—the kind with the shallow charcoal pan and no lid—she dodged flare-ups like a ballet dancer and turned out many batches of perfectly cooked chicken, sticky with barbecue sauce.

Serves **6 to 8** • Prep time **10 mins** • Rest time **5 mins**

2 whole chickens, each about 4 to 4½lb (1.8 to 2kg)

6 tbsp unsalted butter, melted

seasoned salt

low-carb barbecue sauce

1. Preheat the grill to 350°F (177°C).

2. Cut each chicken into 8 pieces: 2 wings, 2 breasts, 2 legs, 2 thighs. Rinse under cold running water and pat dry with paper towels. Place on a rimmed sheet pan. Brush with butter and season with seasoned salt.

3. Place the chicken skin side down on the grate and grill for 30 minutes. Turn and continue to grill until the internal temperature in the thickest part of a breast or a thigh reaches 165°F (74°C), about 45 minutes to 1 hour. During the last 10 minutes, brush the chicken with barbecue sauce.

4. Transfer the chicken to a platter. Serve with additional barbecue sauce.

Nutrition per 2 pieces
Calories **1422** • Total fat **103g** • Carbs **4g** • Dietary fiber **0g** • Sugars **1g** • Protein **113g**

Chicken Cordon Bleu Rollups

apple WOOD PELLETS

400°F (204°C) GRILL TEMP

30 mins COOK TIME

Chicken cordon bleu first appeared in Switzerland in the 1940s and was named after the blue ribbons worn by French knights. Usually breaded and deep fried, this version is much lighter. The chicken is especially attractive if sliced into rounds with a serrated knife before serving.

Serves **8** • Prep time **10 mins** • Rest time **3 mins**

4 boneless, skinless chicken breasts, each about 6 to 8oz (170 to 225g)

garlic salt

freshly ground black pepper

8 thin slices of Swiss cheese

8 thin slices of deli ham or prosciutto

4 tbsp unsalted butter, melted

minced fresh parsley or chives

1. Preheat the grill to 400°F (204°C).

2. Place each chicken breast between two sheets of plastic wrap and pound with a meat mallet or a rolling pin until each breast is ¼ inch (.5cm) thick. Place the breasts smooth side down on a workspace and lightly season with garlic salt and pepper. Top each breast with 2 slices of cheese and 2 slices of ham. Roll up the breasts and secure them with toothpicks that have been coated with vegetable oil. Brush the outside of the breasts with butter and lightly season with garlic salt and pepper.

3. Place the chicken rollups on the grate at an angle to the bars. Smoke for 25 to 30 minutes.

4. Transfer the rollups to a platter and let rest for 3 minutes. Remove the toothpicks. Scatter parsley over the top before serving.

TIPS | *For a different presentation, slice all the rollups (an electric or serrated knife works best) into ¼-inch (.5cm) rounds and place them on a platter. Garnish with the fresh herbs. I suggest **Rainbow Carrots** as a side dish (see page 162).*

Nutrition per ½ rollup

Calories **775** • Total fat **23g** • Carbs **2g** • Dietary fiber **0g** • Sugars **0g** • Protein **131g**

Turkey & Bacon Kebabs
with Ranch-Style Dressing

hickory or oak
WOOD PELLETS

375°F (191°C)
GRILL TEMP

23 to 25 mins
COOK TIME

When sliced crosswise, turkey tenders are the perfect size for kebabs. If you can't find them at your meat counter, buy turkey breast. You might have to trim off the skin and rib bones before cutting the meat into cubes. If you're a fan of dark meat, buy turkey thighs.

Serves **8** • Prep time **25 mins** • Rest time **2 mins**

1½lb (680g) skinless turkey tenders or boneless, skinless turkey breasts, cut into 1-inch (2.5cm) chunks

8 strips of thick-cut bacon

12 fresh bay leaves (optional)

for the dressing

1 cup reduced-fat mayo

1 cup light sour cream

½ cup buttermilk or whole milk, plus more

2 tbsp minced fresh parsley

2 tbsp minced fresh chives

1 tbsp minced fresh dill

2 tsp freshly squeezed lemon juice

1 tsp Worcestershire sauce

1 tsp garlic salt

1 tsp onion powder

½ tsp coarse salt, plus more

½ tsp freshly ground black pepper, plus more

1. In a large bowl, make the dressing by whisking together the mayo, sour cream, and buttermilk until smooth. Whisk in the remaining ingredients. Pour half the mixture into a small bowl. Cover and refrigerate.

2. Add the turkey to the mixture remaining in the bowl and toss to coat thoroughly. If the dressing seems too thick (dip-like), add more buttermilk 1 tablespoon at a time. Cover and refrigerate for 2 to 4 hours.

3. Preheat the grill to 375°F (191°C).

4. Place the bacon on the grate and cook until some of the fat has rendered and the bacon begins to brown, about 15 minutes. Remove the bacon from the grill to cool. Cut the bacon into 1-inch (2.5cm) squares. Set aside.

5. Drain the tenders and discard any excess dressing. Alternate threading the turkey, bacon pieces, and 3 bay leaves on a bamboo skewer. Repeat the threading with 3 more skewers.

6. Place the kebabs on the grate and grill until the turkey is cooked through, about 4 to 5 minutes per side, turning as needed.

7. Transfer the skewers to a platter. Serve with the reserved dressing.

TIPS | *If you lack the fresh herbs to make the dressing, substitute dry herbs, using half the amount called for. Or—even easier—buy a bottle of your favorite ranch dressing at the supermarket.*

Nutrition per ½ kebab

Calories **887** • Total fat **69g** • Carbs **5g** • Dietary fiber **0g** • Sugars **1g** • Protein **58g**

Spiced Cornish Hens
with Cilantro Chutney

Developed in 1950 when Cornish chickens were bred with other breeds, the small birds became a symbol of elegant dining. They're leaner than chicken, with milder-tasting meat. Here, they're brined, stuffed with aromatics, smoke-roasted, and served with an Indian-inspired chutney.

pecan or cherry
WOOD PELLETS

350°F (177°C)
GRILL TEMP

1 hr
COOK TIME

Serves **2** • Prep time **20 mins** • Rest time **5 mins**

2 Cornish game hens, each about 1 to 1¼lb (450 to 565g), thawed if frozen

1 small white onion, peeled and halved

4 slices of fresh ginger

4 garlic cloves, peeled

3 tbsp vegetable oil

2 tsp garam masala

for the brine

½ gallon (1.9 liters) distilled water

½ cup kosher salt

for the chutney

1 bunch of cilantro, washed and roughly chopped

4 scallions, trimmed and roughly chopped

2 garlic cloves, peeled and roughly chopped

2 small green chili peppers, deseeded and minced

1-inch (2.5cm) piece of fresh ginger, peeled and minced

1 tbsp dry-roasted peanuts

1 tsp coarse salt

1 tsp ground cumin

½ tsp ground coriander

3 tbsp freshly squeezed lemon juice

¼ cup extra virgin olive oil

1. In a stockpot on the stovetop over medium-high heat, make the brine by bringing the water and salt to a boil. Stir until the salt dissolves. Remove the pot from the stovetop and let the brine cool to room temperature. Cover and refrigerate until cool.

2. Submerge the hens in the brine. If they float, place a resealable bag of ice on top. Cover and refrigerate for 4 hours or as long as 8 hours.

3. Preheat the grill to 350°F (177°C).

4. In a blender, make the chutney by combining all the ingredients except the olive oil. Blend until the ingredients begin to move, adding 1 tablespoon of water if they need help. When a paste has formed, add the olive oil in a thin stream until the chutney is smooth. If it seems too thick, add a small bit of water. If it's too thin, add a little more oil. Store in a covered container in the refrigerator until ready to use.

5. Remove the hens from the brine. Rinse inside and out under cold running water and pat dry with paper towels. Place half an onion, 2 slices of ginger, and 2 garlic cloves in the cavity of each hen. Tie the legs together with butcher's twine.

6. In a small bowl, combine the vegetable oil and garam masala. Rub the mixture thinly and evenly on the outside of the hens.

7. Place the hens on the grate and roast until they're nicely browned and the internal temperature in the thickest part of a thigh reaches 165°F (74°C), about 1 hour.

8. Transfer the hens to a platter. Serve with the chutney.

Nutrition per 1 hen

Calories **1399** • Total fat **112g** • Carbs **15g** • Dietary fiber **4g** • Sugars **5g** • Protein **82g**

Asian Chicken Sliders

cherry or maple
WOOD PELLETS

450°F (232°C)
GRILL TEMP

8 to 10 mins
COOK TIME

At a time when outrageously sized burgers have become the norm, it's good to know sliders have been holding their own since 1921. A blend of light and dark meat keeps these ground chicken burgers moist. You can find sambal oelek, an Asian chili sauce, in most larger supermarkets.

Serves **4** • Prep time **20 mins** • Rest time **none**

1½lb (680g) ground chicken, preferably a mix of breast and thigh meat

1 large egg, beaten

½ cup panko breadcrumbs or crushed chicharróns

2 scallions, trimmed, white and green parts finely minced

2 garlic cloves, peeled and finely minced

¼ cup loosely packed minced cilantro leaves

2 tbsp sambal oelek

1 tbsp light soy sauce

2 tsp peeled and minced fresh ginger

1 tsp coarse salt

1 tsp freshly ground black pepper

vegetable oil

for serving

8 slider buns

reduced-fat mayo

fresh baby arugula or spinach leaves

pickled onions (optional)

1. Preheat the grill to 450°F (232°C).

2. In a large bowl, combine all the ingredients except the vegetable oil. Wet your hands with cold water. Knead the mixture until it's somewhat sticky and the ingredients are incorporated. Form the mixture into 8 equal-sized patties. Lightly oil the patties on both sides with the oil.

3. Place the patties on the grate and grill until the internal temperature reaches 165°F (74°C), about 4 to 5 minutes per side.

4. Transfer each patty to the bottom half of each bun. Top with a dollop of mayo, a few arugula or spinach leaves, and drained pickled onions (if using). Top each slider with the top half of the bun. Run a knotted bamboo skewer through the top of each slider before serving.

TIPS | *The raw chicken mixture can also be turned into meatloaf or meatballs. Preheat the grill to 350°F (177°C). Adjust the cooking time accordingly to reach the internal temperature of 165°F (74°C). The sliders are also excellent topped with* **Peanut Sauce** *(page 25) or mayo mixed with wasabi. If you're avoiding bread, serve the sliders in butter lettuce leaves.*

Nutrition per 2 sliders

Calories **315** • Total fat **14g** • Carbs **5g** • Dietary fiber **1g** • Sugars **1g** • Protein **39g**

Tandoori Chicken Leg Quarters

An Indian acquaintance used to make wonderful tandoori chicken for parties. Named for ceramic urn-shaped ovens used in India, the dish originated in modern-day Pakistan in the 1940s, although archaeologists have discovered evidence of a similar dish dating to 3000 BCE.

oak
WOOD PELLETS

400°F (204°C)
GRILL TEMP

35 to 40 mins
COOK TIME

Serves **4** • Prep time **20 mins** • Rest time **2 mins**

4 skinless chicken leg quarters, about 2½lb (1.2kg) total

juice of 2 lemons

¼ cup cold distilled water

1½ tsp coarse salt

½ tsp ground turmeric

3 tbsp vegetable oil, plus more

3 garlic cloves, peeled and minced

1½-inch (3.75cm) piece of fresh ginger, peeled and minced

2 tsp sweet paprika

1 tsp chili powder, preferably Kashmiri

1 tsp ground coriander

1 tsp ground cumin

½ tsp ground cayenne

¼ tsp ground nutmeg

½ cup plain Greek yogurt

4 tbsp unsalted butter, melted

for serving

1 large red onion, peeled and thinly sliced crosswise

½ cup cilantro leaves

lemon wedges

1. Use a sharp, thin-bladed knife to cut several deep slashes in the fleshy side of each leg quarter to increase the surface area exposed to the marinade and to help the chicken cook faster. Place the chicken legs in a resealable plastic bag.

2. In a small bowl, combine the lemon juice, water, salt, and turmeric. Stir until the salt dissolves. Pour the mixture over the chicken legs and massage the bag to thoroughly coat the chicken, forcing the liquid into the slashes. Refrigerate for 15 minutes.

3. In a medium bowl, combine the vegetable oil, garlic, ginger, paprika, chili powder, coriander, cumin, cayenne, and nutmeg. Whisk in the yogurt. Add this mixture to the plastic bag and again massage the bag to thoroughly coat the chicken legs. Refrigerate for 4 to 8 hours.

4. Preheat the grill to 400°F (204°C).

5. Remove the chicken from the plastic bag and discard the marinade. Place the leg quarters fleshy side down on the grate and grill until the chicken is nicely browned and the temperature in the thickest part of the thigh reaches 170°F (77°C), about 35 to 40 minutes, turning once or twice.

6. Remove the chicken leg quarters from the grill and let rest for 2 minutes. Brush on both sides with butter. Place the legs on a platter. Scatter the red onion, cilantro leaves, and lemon wedges on the platter. Serve immediately.

TIPS | *Indian restaurants often serve tandoori chicken that's luridly orange-red. Originally made from dried insects, today's food dyes are usually vegetal in nature. Feel free to use red or orange food dyes in the marinade if you desire the carmine color. For a low-carb side dish, serve cauliflower rice and/or slices of grilled eggplant.*

Nutrition per 8oz (225g)
Calories **482** • Total fat **38g** • Carbs **0g** • Dietary fiber **0g** • Sugars **0g** • Protein **38g**

Spatchcocked Chicken
with White Barbecue Sauce

Smoked chicken with white barbecue sauce started at Big Bob Gibson Bar-B-Q in Decatur, Alabama. He dipped smoked chickens in this mayo- and vinegar-based sauce when he opened his restaurant in 1925—perhaps to keep them moist after they emerged from the pit.

hickory
WOOD PELLETS

325°F (163°C)
GRILL TEMP

1 hr
COOK TIME

Serves **4** • Prep time **20 mins** • Rest time **5 mins**

1 whole chicken, about 4 to 4½lb (1.8 to 2kg), preferably organic or farm raised

extra virgin olive oil

White Barbecue Sauce (page 24)

chopped fresh chives (optional)

for the brine

½ gallon (1.9 liters) distilled water

½ cup kosher salt

2 tbsp light brown sugar or low-carb substitute

for the rub

¼ cup coarse salt

¼ cup granulated light brown sugar or low-carb substitute

¼ cup sweet or smoked paprika

2 tbsp freshly ground black pepper

1 tbsp granulated garlic

2 tsp dried thyme

½ tsp ground cayenne

1. In a large stockpot on the stovetop over medium-high heat, make the brine by combining the ingredients. Bring the mixture to a boil. Stir until the salt and sugar dissolve. Remove the pot from the stovetop and let the brine cool to room temperature. Cover and refrigerate until cool.

2. Remove the backbone of the chicken by using a sharp knife, starting at the tail and cutting through the rib bones. Repeat on the other side of the backbone. Fold the two halves backward to release the cartilaginous breastbone. (You might have to use a knife to slice through the thin skin on either side.) Remove the breastbone. Turn the chicken over and gently flatten it with the palm of your hand. Submerge the chicken in the brine. If it floats, place a resealable bag of ice on top. Refrigerate for 4 to 6 hours.

3. Preheat the grill to 325°F (163°C).

4. In a small bowl, make the rub by combining the ingredients.

5. Rinse the chicken with cold running water and dry with paper towels. (Discard the brine.) Coat the skin with olive oil. Lightly dust the chicken on both sides with the rub. (Save the remainder for another grill session.) Tuck the wingtips behind the chicken's back.

6. Place the chicken ribs side down on the grate and grill until the skin is nicely browned and the internal temperature in a thigh reaches 170°F (77°C), about 1 hour.

7. Transfer the chicken to a platter. Spoon the white barbecue sauce over the chicken. Spread the sauce with a basting brush, letting it pool in places. Lightly scatter the chives over the top. Carve the chicken and serve with extra sauce on the side.

Nutrition per 3oz (170g)
Calories **749** • Total fat **61g** • Carbs **12g** • Dietary fiber **2g** • Sugars **10g** • Protein **39g**

Thai Chicken Satays

With origins in Indonesia, satay ("stick meat") is considered a variant of Japanese yakitori, Turkish shish kebab, and South African sosatie. It's often chargrilled on makeshift braziers or mangals—narrow grateless grills that support the ends of the skewers on parallel rails.

cherry
WOOD PELLETS

450°F (232°C)
GRILL TEMP

6 to 10 mins
COOK TIME

Serves **4** • Prep time **20 mins** • Rest time **none**

1½lb (680g) boneless, skinless chicken breasts

for the marinade
½ cup unsweetened canned light coconut milk

2 garlic cloves, peeled and coarsely chopped

¼ cup loosely packed fresh cilantro leaves

1-inch (2.5cm) piece of fresh ginger, peeled and coarsely chopped

2 tbsp light soy sauce

1 tbsp Asian fish sauce

1 tbsp light brown sugar or low-carb substitute

2 tsp sambal oelek (optional)

1 tsp Thai-style curry powder

1 tsp ground cumin

1 tsp ground turmeric

1 tsp coarse salt

2 tbsp vegetable oil

for serving
butter lettuce leaves, washed and dried

cherry tomatoes

Peanut Sauce (page 25)

1. Use a sharp knife to slice the chicken breasts lengthwise into strips, each about 1 inch (2.5cm) wide. (If the chicken breasts are unusually thick, butterfly them before cutting them into strips.) Place the breasts in a resealable plastic bag.

2. In a blender, make the marinade by combining the ingredients. Blend until fairly smooth. Pour the marinade over the chicken, turning and massaging the bag to thoroughly coat the chicken. Refrigerate for 2 hours.

3. Preheat the grill to 450°F (232°C).

4. Remove the chicken from the marinade and let any excess drip off. (Discard the marinade.) Thread each chicken strip on a bamboo skewer, pushing the point in one side of the chicken and out the other as if sewing. Leave very little of the tip exposed because it will burn easily.

5. Place the skewers on the grate perpendicular to the bars. Grill until the chicken has grill marks and is fully cooked, about 3 to 5 minutes per side.

6. Remove the skewers from the grill. Place the lettuce leaves on a platter. Place the satays atop the leaves. Scatter cherry tomatoes over the top. Serve with the peanut sauce.

TIPS | *Feel free to substitute pork loin (or even tofu) for chicken in this recipe. Coconut milk tends to separate, so shake the can vigorously before measuring the milk. If the handle ends of the skewers begin to scorch—soaking them in water doesn't seem to make a difference in my experience—slip a folded sheet of aluminum foil under them.*

Nutrition per 5 satays
Calories **215** • Total fat **6g** • Carbs **2g** • Dietary fiber **0g** • Sugars **1g** • Protein **36g**

Cider-Brined Turkey

Soaking your turkey in heavily salted water does magical things to it. Brining denatures (unwinds) the proteins in the meat, leaving it moist and tender even when cooked over the high dry heat of the grill. Make sure you buy a bird that hasn't already been injected with broth.

apple
WOOD PELLETS

350°F (177°C)
GRILL TEMP

2½ to 3 hrs
COOK TIME

Serves **8** • Prep time **20 mins** • Rest time **20 mins**

1 whole turkey, about 12 to 14lb (4.5 to 5.4kg), thawed if frozen

1 white onion, peeled and sliced into quarters

1 apple, cut into wedges

2 celery stalks, sliced into 2-inch (5cm) pieces

sprigs of fresh sage, rosemary, parsley, or thyme

8 tbsp unsalted butter, at room temperature

coarse salt

freshly ground black pepper

for the brine

1 quart (1 liter) apple cider or apple juice

3 quarts (3 liters) cold distilled water

¾ cup coarse salt

½ cup light brown sugar or low-carb substitute

3 garlic cloves, peeled and smashed with a chef's knife

3 bay leaves

1. In a large food-safe bucket, make the brine by combining the apple cider, water, salt, and brown sugar. Stir until the salt and sugar dissolve. Add the garlic and bay leaves. Submerge the turkey in the brine. If it floats, place a resealable bag of ice on top. Refrigerate for at least 8 hours and up to 16 hours.

2. Preheat the grill to 350°F (177°C).

3. Remove the turkey from the brine and pat dry with paper towels. Discard the brine. Place the onion, apple, celery, and herbs in the main cavity. Tie the legs together with butcher's twine. Fold the wings behind the back. Rub the outside with butter. Lightly season with salt and pepper.

4. Place the turkey breast side up on a wire rack in a shallow roasting pan. Place the pan on the grate and roast the turkey until the internal temperature in the thickest part of a thigh reaches 165°F (74°C), about 2½ to 3 hours.

5. Transfer the turkey to a cutting board and let rest for 20 minutes. (Save the drippings to make from-scratch turkey gravy.) Carve the turkey and arrange the meat on a large platter before serving.

TIPS | If your turkey is frozen, allow at least 24 hours per every 5 pounds (2.3kg) to thaw it in the refrigerator. Aluminum foil roasting pans make clean-up easier but are sometimes too flimsy to hold the weight of the bird without buckling. Buy the most substantial foil roasting pans you can find and then double up on them. Use the second one for leftovers.

Nutrition per 4oz (170g)

Calories **534** • Total fat **24g** • Carbs **0g** • Dietary fiber **0g** • Sugars **0g** • Protein **75g**

Roasted Duck
with Cherry Salsa

cherry, apple,
or another
fruitwood
WOOD PELLETS

350°F (177°C)
GRILL TEMP

3 hrs
COOK TIME

Over the years, I've tried many tricks to achieve a crisp, lacquered skin on duck. But I've learned that a long roast, during which you flip the duck during the cook, is the easiest way to produce that visually appealing skin. Serve the duck with a garnet-colored cherry salsa.

Serves **2 to 3** • Prep time **15 mins** • Rest time **15 mins**

1 whole Long Island (Pekin) duck, about 5 to 6lb (2.3 to 2.7kg), thawed if frozen

coarse salt

freshly ground black pepper

1 white onion, peeled and quartered

1 orange, quartered

4 garlic cloves, peeled and quartered

3 sprigs of fresh thyme or fresh rosemary, plus more

for the salsa

2 cups dark red cherries, washed, destemmed, pitted, and coarsely chopped

1 scallion, trimmed, white and green parts sliced crosswise

1 jalapeño, destemmed, deseeded, and finely diced

1 tbsp granulated sugar, plus more

1 tbsp port wine (optional)

2 tsp freshly squeezed lime juice

2 tsp freshly squeezed orange juice

1½ tsp finely chopped orange zest

1. Preheat the grill to 350°F (177°C).

2. In a small bowl, make the salsa by combining the ingredients. Slightly bruise some of the cherries to release their juices. Set aside.

3. Use kitchen shears to cut off the wing tips and trim any excessive neck skin from the duck. Use a sharp knife to score the skin of the breasts in the classic diamond pattern, making the cuts about 1 inch (2.5cm) apart, but don't penetrate the meat. Use a fork with sharp tines to prick the skin on the thighs. Rinse the bird inside and out with cold running water and pat dry with paper towels.

4. Season the duck inside and out with the salt and pepper. Tuck the onion, orange, garlic, and thyme in the cavity. Pull the excess skin over the opening and tie the legs together with butcher's twine.

5. Place a wire rack in a shallow roasting pan and place the duck breast side up on top of the rack. Place the roasting pan on the grate and roast the duck for 1 hour. Use tongs to turn the bird breast side down. Roast for 1 hour more and then turn again, finishing breast side up. Roast until the skin is nicely browned and the internal temperature in the thickest part of a breast reaches 170°F (77°C), about 30 minutes to 1 hour more. (There should also be quite a bit of duck fat in the bottom of the pan. Save in a covered container and refrigerate or freeze for another use.)

6. Remove the pan from the grill and let the duck rest for 15 minutes. Transfer the duck to a cutting board and carve.

7. Place the duck meat on a platter and scatter the fresh thyme over the top. Serve with the cherry salsa.

Nutrition per 3oz (170g)
Calories **1301** • Total fat **87g** • Carbs **29g** • Dietary fiber **4g** • Sugars **20g** • Protein **101g**

Yucatán-Spiced Chicken Thighs

Achiote paste—also called *recado rojo*—gives a spicy kick and tandoori-like orangish-red color to food, especially these chicken thighs. For even more heat, add a spoonful of adobo sauce (the kind chipotle peppers are canned with). The marinade for the chicken is also good on pork.

mesquite or oak
WOOD PELLETS

400°F (204°C)
GRILL TEMP

35 to 40 mins
COOK TIME

Serves **4** • Prep time **15 mins** • Rest time **none**

8 skin-on, bone-in chicken thighs, about 2½lb (1.2kg) total

for the marinade
2oz (55g) achiote paste
¼ cup hot distilled water
¼ cup freshly squeezed orange juice
2 tbsp freshly squeezed lime juice
2 tbsp apple cider vinegar or distilled white vinegar
2 tbsp vegetable oil or extra virgin olive oil
2 garlic cloves, peeled and minced
1 tsp kosher salt, plus more
1 tsp dried Mexican oregano
½ tsp ground cumin
¼ tsp ground cinnamon

1. In a small bowl, make the marinade by using a fork to crumble the achiote paste. Add the hot water and mash the paste with the fork until blended. Whisk in the orange juice, lime juice, vinegar, oil, garlic, salt, oregano, cumin, and cinnamon.

2. Place the chicken thighs in a resealable plastic bag. Pour the marinade over the chicken, turning and massaging the bag to thoroughly coat the chicken. Refrigerate for 2 hours.

3. Preheat the grill to 400°F (204°C).

4. Remove the chicken thighs from the marinade and let any excess drip off. (Discard the marinade.) Place the chicken thighs skin side down on the grate at an angle to the bars. Grill for 20 minutes and then turn. Continue to grill until the internal temperature in the thighs reaches 165°F (74°C), about 20 minutes more.

5. Transfer the thighs to a platter and serve immediately.

TIPS | *Achiote paste is a popular seasoning in the Yucatán and comes in a small brick. It's made from crushed annatto seeds as well as salt, cumin, oregano, and other spices. If you can't find it at your local market, it's available online.*

Nutrition per 2 thighs
Calories **330** • Total fat **22g** • Carbs **1g** • Dietary fiber **0g** • Sugars **1g** • Protein **31g**

Bourbon-Brined Turkey Thighs

Craving the flavors of Thanksgiving but don't want to deal with cooking a whole bird? Turkey thighs (and breasts, for that matter) are usually available throughout the year. Finishing the thighs at a higher temperature will ensure the skin will crisp as it renders its fat.

pecan, hickory, or oak
WOOD PELLETS

250°F (121°C); 375°F (191°C)
GRILL TEMP

120 to 135 mins
COOK TIME

Serves **4** • Prep time **15 mins** • Rest time **3 mins**

4 skin-on, bone-in turkey thighs, about 2lb (1kg) total

6 tbsp unsalted butter, at room temperature

4 large fresh sage leaves

coarse salt

freshly ground black pepper

for the brine

1 quart (1 liter) distilled water

¼ cup coarse salt, plus more

¼ cup light brown sugar or low-carb substitute

¼ cup bourbon (optional)

1. In a saucepan on the stovetop over medium-high heat, make the brine by combining the water, salt, brown sugar, and bourbon (if using). Bring to a boil. Stir until the salt and sugar dissolve. Remove the saucepan from the stovetop and let the brine cool to room temperature.

2. Place the turkey in a resealable plastic bag and pour the brine over the thighs. Refrigerate for 4 hours.

3. Preheat the grill to 250°F (121°C).

4. Drain the turkey thighs and discard the brine. Rinse under cold running water and pat dry with paper towels. Gently lift the skin of each thigh and push 2 teaspoons of butter underneath. Top the butter with a sage leaf, smoothing it out so it lays flat under the skin. Rub the outside of the skin with more butter. Lightly season with salt and pepper

5. Place the turkey thighs on the grate at an angle to the bars. Smoke for 1½ hours. Raise the temperature to 375°F (191°C) and roast until the skin is golden brown and the internal temperature in the thickest part of the meat reaches 170°F (77°C), about 30 to 45 minutes.

6. Transfer the thighs to a platter. Let rest for 3 minutes before serving.

TIPS | *If you're short on time, you can skip the brine. While some people oil the skin of the bird, the solids in the butter will lead to better browning.*

Nutrition per 1 thigh

Calories **603** • Total fat **38g** • Carbs **2g** • Dietary fiber **0g** • Sugars **2g** • Protein **59g**

Chicken on a Throne

I was once hired to style food for some TV appearances by Steven Raichlen, who was promoting his book, *Beer-Can Chicken*. The first appearance was at 6 a.m. So I stayed up all night grilling the perfect beer can chicken. Make sure there's enough clearance under your grill lid to accommodate the bird and its "throne."

hickory, oak, or pecan
WOOD PELLETS

350°F (177°C)
GRILL TEMP

1 to 1¼ hrs
COOK TIME

Serves **6** • Prep time **10 mins** • Rest time **5 mins**

1 can of low-carb beer or sugar-free dark-colored soda, about 12oz (350ml)

1 whole chicken, about 4lb (1.8kg)

3 tbsp barbecue rub, plus more

1. Preheat the grill to 350°F (177°C).

2. Pour half the contents of the can into a glass for drinking. Set the half-full can aside.

3. Blot any juices off the chicken with paper towels. Sprinkle 2 teaspoons of the rub in the body and neck cavities. Sprinkle the remaining rub evenly on the outside. Tuck the wing tips behind the bird's back.

4. Carefully lower the chicken (body cavity side down) over the can. Place the chicken upright on its can on the grate. (For stability, pull the legs forward and rest them on the grate to essentially form a tripod.) Roast the chicken until the internal temperature in the thickest part of a thigh reaches 165°F (74°C), about 1 hour. (Check on your bird periodically to make sure it hasn't tipped over.) If it hasn't yet reached that temperature, continue cooking for about 15 minutes more.

5. Use heavy-duty insulated rubber gloves and tongs to carefully transfer the chicken to the kitchen. Let rest 5 minutes and then carefully ease the chicken off the can. Discard the can and its steaming liquid, being careful not to burn yourself. Carve the chicken and serve.

Nutrition per ⅙ chicken
Calories **669** • Total fat **45g** • Carbs **2g** • Dietary fiber **0g** • Sugars **0g** • Protein **56g**

Grilled Salmon Gravlax

Inspiration for this dish came from Scandinavian gravlax—salmon cured with salt, sugar, and fistfuls of fresh dill and then eaten raw. And it's wonderful—quite a delicacy. But it's even better when grilled, kissed with a hint of wood smoke. Serve as a main course or as an appetizer.

alder
WOOD PELLETS

400°F (204°C)
GRILL TEMP

6 to 10 mins
COOK TIME

Serves **4** • Prep time **20 mins** • Rest time **none**

1 center-cut salmon fillet, about 2lb (1kg), preferably wild caught, skin on

½ cup aquavit or vodka

4 whole juniper berries

¼ cup finely chopped fresh dill, plus more

lemon wedges

for the rub

3 tbsp granulated light brown sugar or low-carb substitute

2 tbsp coarse salt

2 tsp freshly ground black pepper

1 tsp freshly ground white pepper

1 tsp ground coriander

1. Run your fingers over the fillet, feeling for bones. Remove them with kitchen tweezers or needle-nosed pliers. Rinse the salmon under cold running water and pat dry with paper towels.

2. Place the salmon skin side down in a nonreactive baking dish and pour the aquavit over it. Crush the berries with the flat of a chef's knife and add them to the dish. Cover and refrigerate for 1 hour.

3. In a small bowl, make the rub by combining the ingredients.

4. Remove the salmon from the aquavit and pat dry with paper towels. Discard the soaking liquid and juniper berries. Rinse out the baking dish and place the salmon in the dish. Lightly but evenly sprinkle the rub on the flesh side of the fillet and gently distribute it with your fingertips. Scatter the dill over the top. Cover the dish and refrigerate for 4 hours.

5. Preheat the grill to 400°F (204°C).

6. With a sharp knife, slice the fillet into 4 equal portions. Place the fillets on the grate and grill until the fish is somewhat opaque but still translucent in the center and the internal temperature reaches 125°F (52°C), about 3 to 5 minutes per side.

7. Transfer the fillets to a platter. Scatter more dill over the top. Serve with lemon wedges.

Nutrition per 8oz (225g)
Calories **428** • Total fat **20g** • Carbs **10g** • Dietary fiber **1g** • Sugars **9g** • Protein **49g**

Grilled Tilapia
with Blistered Cherry Tomatoes

Ten years ago, few people had heard of tilapia, a fish native to Africa. Today, Americans eat more than 475 million pounds of this lean, mild-tasting white fish. Be sure to brush your grill grate with oil before cooking because delicate fish fillets have a tendency to stick.

alder or oak
WOOD PELLETS

400°F (204°C)
GRILL TEMP

13 to 15 mins
COOK TIME

Serves **4** • Prep time **10 mins** • Rest time **none**

1½lb (680g) tilapia fillets or other mild white fish fillets

chopped fresh curly or flat-leaf parsley

for the marinade
½ cup extra virgin olive oil

1 garlic clove, peeled and smashed with a chef's knife

3 tbsp freshly squeezed lemon juice

1 tsp smoked paprika

½ tsp coarse salt

¼ tsp freshly ground black pepper

for the tomatoes
2 tbsp extra virgin olive oil

2 pints (1 liter) cherry tomatoes (red, yellow, or heirloom varieties)

coarse salt

freshly ground black pepper

1. Place a cast iron skillet on the grate. Preheat the grill to 400°F (204°C).

2. In a jar with a tight-fitting lid, make the marinade by combining the ingredients. Shake the jar vigorously to emulsify the ingredients.

3. Place the fillets in a single layer in a nonreactive baking dish. Pour half the marinade over them and turn the fillets to thoroughly coat. Cover with plastic wrap and refrigerate for 15 minutes. (Refrigerate no more than 30 minutes or the acid in the marinade will begin to cook the fish.)

4. Place the olive oil in the skillet. Add the tomatoes and season with salt and pepper. Stir to coat. Cook the tomatoes until they begin to blister and collapse, about 5 minutes, stirring once or twice. Remove the skillet from the grill and transfer the tomatoes to a bowl.

5. Carefully lift each fish fillet from the marinade and let the excess drip off. Place the fillets on the grate at a slight angle to the bars. Lightly season with salt and pepper. Grill until the fish flakes easily when pressed with a fork, about 4 to 5 minutes per side, turning carefully with a thin-bladed spatula.

6. Transfer the fillets to a warmed platter. Top with some of the tomatoes. (Place the remaining tomatoes in a serving bowl.) Scatter the parsley around the platter. Drizzle some of the remaining marinade over the top. Serve immediately.

TIPS | *Good substitutes for tilapia include orange roughy, trout, or red snapper fillets. Actually, you can use nearly any non-oily fish fillets—or even fish steaks, such as tuna or swordfish—in this recipe. (You might need to adjust cooking times depending on the thickness of the fish.) The marinade and tomatoes would complement any of them. Complete the meal with a green salad and a crisp white wine.*

Nutrition per 6oz (110g) fish and 1 cup tomatoes
Calories **293** • Total fat **16g** • Carbs **5g** • Dietary fiber **2g** • Sugars **3g** • Protein **34g**

Thai-Style Swordfish Steaks
with Peanut Sauce

alder
WOOD PELLETS

450°F (232°C)
GRILL TEMP

6 to 8 mins
COOK TIME

The vibrant cuisine of Thailand is characterized by the masterful interplay of salty, sweet, sour, and spicy. Here, meaty swordfish steaks marinate in coconut milk spiced with ginger, garlic, and chili pepper before being grilled over high heat and served with a peanut sauce.

Serves **4** • Prep time **20 mins** • Rest time **5 mins**

4 center-cut swordfish steaks, each about 6oz (170g) and 1 inch (2.5cm) thick

Peanut Sauce (page 25)

lime wedges

for the marinade

½ cup light Thai-style unsweetened coconut milk

2 garlic cloves, peeled and smashed with a chef's knife

juice and zest of 1 lime

1-inch (2.5cm) piece of fresh ginger, peeled and roughly chopped

½ Thai bird's eye chili pepper or serrano pepper, deseeded and thinly sliced, plus more

2 tbsp fresh cilantro leaves, coarsely chopped

1 tbsp Asian fish sauce

1 tbsp light soy sauce or liquid aminos

1 tbsp light brown sugar or low-carb substitute

1 tsp ground coriander

½ tsp ground turmeric

1. In a medium bowl, make the marinade by whisking together the ingredients. Whisk until the brown sugar dissolves.

2. Place the swordfish steaks in a single layer in a nonreactive baking dish and pour the marinade over them, turning the steaks to coat thoroughly. Refrigerate for 1 hour.

3. Preheat the grill to 450°F (232°C).

4. Remove the swordfish from the marinade and scrape off any solids. (Discard the marinade.) Place the steaks on the grate and grill until the fish easily flakes when pressed with a fork, about 3 to 4 minutes per side, turning with a thin-bladed spatula.

5. Transfer the swordfish steaks to a platter. Serve with the peanut sauce and lime wedges.

TIPS | *If you have leftover peanut sauce, use it on grilled pork or chicken or as a dip for raw vegetables.*

Nutrition per 1 swordfish steak and ¼ cup peanut sauce

Calories **481** • Total fat **31g** • Carbs **14g** • Dietary fiber **3g** • Sugars **5g** • Protein **40g**

Grilled Lobster Tails
with Smoked Paprika Butter

Whether served alone or as part of a decadent "surf and turf" menu, lobster is a celebratory special occasion meat. Once you've eaten it grilled, you won't want it boiled or steamed again. The subtle smoke flavor is reinforced by the smoked paprika that enlivens the butter.

cherry, apple, or another fruitwood
WOOD PELLETS

450°F (232°C)
GRILL TEMP

10 to 12 mins
COOK TIME

Serves **4** • Prep time **15 mins** • Rest time **none**

4 lobster tails, each about 8 to 10oz (225 to 285g), thawed if frozen

3 lemons, 1 quartered lengthwise, 2 halved through their equators

for the butter

1¼ cup unsalted butter, at room temperature

2 garlic cloves, peeled and finely minced

3 tbsp chopped fresh parsley

2 tbsp chopped fresh chives

1 tbsp freshly squeezed lemon juice

2 tsp finely chopped lemon zest

2 tsp smoked paprika

1 tsp coarse salt

1. Preheat the grill to 450°F (232°C).

2. In a medium bowl, make the paprika butter by combining the ingredients. Beat with a wooden spoon until well blended.

3. Use a sharp, heavy knife or sturdy kitchen shears to cut lengthwise through the top shell of each lobster tail in a straight line toward the tail fin. Gently loosen the meat from the bottom shell and sides. Lift the meat through the slit you just made so the meat sits on top of the shell. Slip a lemon quarter underneath the meat (between the meat and the bottom shell) to keep it elevated. Spread 1 tablespoon of paprika butter on top of each lobster. Melt the remaining butter and keep it warm.

4. Place the lobster tails flesh side up and lemon halves cut sides down on the grate. Grill the lobsters until the flesh is white and opaque and the internal temperature of the lobster meat reaches 135 to 140°F (57 to 60°C), about 10 to 12 minutes, basting at least once with some of the melted butter. (Don't overcook or the lobster will become unpleasantly rubbery.)

5. Transfer the lobsters and the lemon halves to a platter. Divide the remaining melted butter between 4 ramekins before serving.

TIP | *For a more attractive presentation of the butter, pour only the clear butter into the ramekins and leave the white milk solids behind.*

Nutrition per 1 lobster tail

Calories **616** • Total fat **50g** • Carbs **4g** • Dietary fiber **1g** • Sugars **4g** • Protein **46g**

Tequila & Lime Shrimp
with Smoked Tomato Sauce

There's no need to break out your finest reposado (tequila aged in oak barrels) or mezcal (distilled smoked agave) to marinate the shrimp, but use an eminently drinkable spirit The spicy tomato sauce also pairs well with grilled scallops, soft-shell crabs, chicken, skirt steak, and pork.

oak or mesquite
WOOD PELLETS

450°F (232°C)
GRILL TEMP

4 to 6 mins
COOK TIME

Serves **4** • Prep time **10 mins** • Rest time **none**

24 to 28 jumbo shrimp, about 2lb (1kg) total, peeled and deveined

1 lime, quartered

Smoked Tomato Sauce (page 24)

for the marinade

½ cup tequila or mezcal

juice and zest of 1 lime

2 garlic cloves, peeled and roughly chopped

½ cup freshly squeezed orange juice

¼ cup extra virgin olive oil

2 tsp agave, light brown sugar, or low-carb substitute

2 tsp Mexican hot sauce, plus more

1½ tsp coarse salt

1 tsp baking soda

1 tsp chili powder

½ tsp ground cumin

1. In a medium bowl, make the marinade by whisking together the ingredients. Whisk until the salt dissolves. Taste for seasoning, adding more hot sauce if desired.

2. Place the shrimp in a resealable plastic bag and pour the marinade over them, turning the bag several times to coat thoroughly. Refrigerate for 30 minutes.

3. Preheat the grill to 450°F (232°C).

4. Drain the shrimp and discard the marinade. Pat the shrimp dry with paper towels. Thread the shrimp on 4 bamboo skewers (preferably flat ones). Make sure all the shrimp face the same direction. Finish each skewer with a lime wedge.

5. Place the skewers on the grate and grill until the shrimp are white and opaque, about 2 to 3 minutes per side, turning once. (Don't overcook.)

6. Remove the shrimp from the grill. Serve immediately with the warm tomato sauce.

Nutrition per 6 to 7 shrimp

Calories **532** • Total fat **23g** • Carbs **29g** • Dietary fiber **7g** • Sugars **18g** • Protein **50g**

Grilled Tuna Steaks
with Lemon & Caper Butter

Sushi-quality tuna steaks are a must for this preparation. The steaks are briefly seared on a screaming hot grill, leaving the interior rosy rare. Because it's so lean, tuna tends to dry out if overcooked. The caper butter offers a rich counterpoint to the tuna.

alder
WOOD PELLETS

450°F (232°C)
GRILL TEMP

6 to 8 mins
COOK TIME

Serves **4** • Prep time **10 mins** • Rest time **5 mins**

4 tuna steaks, each about 8oz (225g) and 1 inch (2.5cm) thick

extra virgin olive oil

coarse salt

freshly ground black pepper

for the butter

6 tbsp unsalted butter, chilled, divided

1 garlic clove, peeled and minced

3 tbsp brined capers, drained and coarsely chopped

1 tbsp freshly squeezed lemon juice, plus more

1 tsp lemon zest

1 tbsp minced fresh chives or flat-leaf parsley

1. Preheat the grill to 450°F (232°C).

2. In a small saucepan on the stovetop over medium-low heat, begin making the butter by melting 1 tablespoon of butter. (Cut the remaining butter into ½-inch (1.25cm) cubes and keep them cold.) Add the garlic and capers. Cook until the garlic is softened, about 3 minutes. Stir in the lemon juice and zest. Remove the saucepan from the heat and set aside.

3. Lightly brush the tuna steaks with olive oil. Season with salt and pepper. Place the steaks on the grate and grill until seared, about 3 to 4 minutes per side. (The tuna will be quite rare in the center, almost like sashimi. If you prefer your tuna more well done, add 4 to 6 minutes to the grilling time.)

4. Transfer the steaks to a platter and let rest for 5 minutes.

5. Reheat the butter and caper mixture over low heat. Whisk in the chilled butter one or two cubes at a time until the sauce has emulsified. Stir in the chives. Ladle the sauce over the tuna. Serve immediately.

TIP | *If desired, grill some asparagus alongside the tuna for an easy side dish. The tuna and asparagus have similar cooking times (6 to 8 minutes) if the spears are fairly thin. Pair with a Sauvignon Blanc, Pinot Noir, or a dry Riesling.*

Nutrition per 1 tuna steak
Calories **370** • Total fat **18g** • Carbs **1g** • Dietary fiber **0g** • Sugars **0g** • Protein **52g**

Oysters Margarita

These oysters are doused with the same ingredients required for a properly made margarita as well as melted butter. Because oysters tend to be "tippy" on the grill (and these might also be a bit "tipsy"), I like to balance them on a special oyster rack. Serve them on a bed of rock salt.

mesquite
WOOD PELLETS

450°F (232°C)
GRILL TEMP

8 to 10 minutes
COOK TIME

Serves **4**   •   Prep time **20 mins**   •   Rest time **none**

24 fresh oysters in the shell

4oz (120ml) freshly squeezed lime juice

2oz (60ml) tequila

2oz (60ml) orange liqueur, such as triple sec

6 tbsp cold butter, cut into 24 cubes

crunchy salt, such as margarita rimming salt

lime wedges

hot sauce (optional)

1. Preheat the grill to 450°F (232°C).

2. Carefully shuck each oyster to remove the top shell. Run your shucking knife under the oyster to release it from the bottom shell, but don't spill the juices. Discard the top shells, but keep the oysters in the bottom shells. Balance each oyster on a wire rack placed on a rimmed sheet pan.

3. Place 1 teaspoon of lime juice, ½ teaspoon of tequila, ½ teaspoon of orange liqueur, and 1 cube of butter on each oyster.

4. Place the pan on the grate and smoke until the butter has melted and the juices are bubbling, about 8 to 10 minutes. (The oysters should be just barely cooked.)

5. Remove the pan from the grill. Sprinkle a pinch of salt on each oyster. Serve immediately with lime wedges and hot sauce (if using).

Nutrition per 6 oysters
Calories **382**   •   Total fat **22g**   •   Carbs **10g**   •   Dietary fiber **0g**   •   Sugars **14g**   •   Protein **17g**

Florentine Shrimp al Cartoccio

oak
WOOD PELLETS

400°F (204°C)
GRILL TEMP

10 to 13 mins
COOK TIME

The French call it *en papillote* and the Italians call it *al cartoccio*. But it means cooking in foil packets. There's a certain thrill in opening a package of food cooked over fire. This dish is also good when chicken cubes replace the shrimp. Increase the cooking time by a few minutes.

Serves **4** • Prep time **15 mins** • Rest time **none**

6 tbsp unsalted butter, melted

½ cup heavy whipping cream

½ cup grated Parmesan cheese

2 garlic cloves, peeled and minced

1 cup thinly sliced button mushrooms, cleaned and destemmed

1 cup baby spinach leaves

2 tbsp chopped sun-dried, oil-packed tomatoes

½ tsp dried oregano

½ tsp dried basil

½ tsp crushed red pepper flakes, plus more

½ tsp coarse salt

½ tsp freshly ground black pepper

20 to 24 jumbo shrimp, about 1lb (450g) total, peeled and deveined

sprigs of fresh rosemary, basil, thyme, or oregano

1. Preheat the grill to 400°F (204°C).

2. In a large bowl, combine the butter and whipping cream. Stir in the Parmesan, garlic, mushrooms, spinach, tomatoes, oregano, basil, red pepper flakes, and salt and pepper. Add the shrimp and stir gently to coat.

3. Place four 12-inch (30.5cm) sheets of wide heavy-duty aluminum foil on a workspace and pull up the sides. Divide the shrimp mixture evenly between the sheets of foil. Roll and crimp the top and sides of the foil to create sealed packages.

4. Place the packets seam side up on the grate and grill until the shrimp are cooked through, about 10 to 13 minutes. (You can carefully open one package to check on the shrimp.)

5. Transfer the packets to plates. Carefully open the packets to avoid any steam. Scatter fresh herbs over the shrimp before serving.

TIPS | *When using dried herbs, rub them between your fingers first to release their oils. Replace every 6 months. Shrimp are properly cooked when they turn pink and opaque and have formed a "C" shape. If they're curled tightly into an "O," they're a bit overcooked.*

Nutrition per 6 shrimp
Calories **258** • Total fat **12g** • Carbs **0g** • Dietary fiber **0g** • Sugars **1g** • Protein **36g**

Hot-Smoked Salmon

Not to be confused with the raw cold-smoked salmon (nova) sold at gourmet markets and delis, this salmon is smoked at a higher temp. This recipe produces a simple but clean-tasting fish with just the right balance of salty, smoky, and sweet. It can be served hot or cold.

alder
WOOD PELLETS

150°F (66°C)
GRILL TEMP

3 hrs
COOK TIME

Serves **4** • Prep time **15 mins** • Rest time **10 mins**

1½lb (680g) skinless center-cut salmon fillet, preferably wild caught

for the brine
1 quart (1 liter) distilled water
¼ cup coarse salt
¼ cup light brown sugar or low-carb equivalent
¼ cup gin (optional)

1. In a saucepan on the stovetop over medium-high heat, make the brine by combining the water, salt, brown sugar, and gin (if using). Bring the mixture to a boil. Stir until the salt and sugar dissolve. Remove the pan from the stovetop and let the brine cool to room temperature. Refrigerate until cool.

2. Run your fingers over the salmon fillet, feeling for bones. Remove any with kitchen tweezers or needle-nosed pliers. Rinse the salmon under cold running water. Place the salmon in a resealable plastic bag and pour the brine over it. Refrigerate for 4 to 8 hours.

3. Place a wire rack on a rimmed sheet pan. Remove the salmon from the brine and rinse under cold running water. Pat dry with paper towels and then place the salmon on the wire rack. Place the pan in a cool area with good air circulation (such as near a fan). In 2 to 4 hours, you'll notice the salmon has developed a pellicle—a kind of sticky skin or coating that will help the smoke adhere to the fish. (Don't skip this step.)

4. Preheat the grill to 150°F (66°C).

5. Place the salmon on the grate and smoke until the fish flakes easily when pressed with a fork and the internal temperature reaches 140°F (60°C), about 3 hours. If albumin (a harmless white protein) appears on top of the fillet as it smokes, gently remove it with a paper towel.

6. Remove the salmon from the grill and let rest for 10 minutes. (You can also transfer the fish to a clean wire rack and let it cool to room temperature. Cover and refrigerate if not using immediately. The salmon will keep for up to 5 days.)

7. Serve the salmon with eggs, on salads, with **Mustard Caviar** (page 26), or with its traditional accompaniments: cream cheese, capers, chopped hard-boiled eggs, diced red onion, and dark bread.

TIPS | *If you prefer that your smoked salmon have a sweeter flavor profile, brush it once or twice during the smoke with warmed maple syrup or honey.*

Nutrition per 6oz (170g)
Calories **385** • Total fat **11g** • Carbs **3g** • Dietary fiber **0g** • Sugars **3g** • Protein **61g**

Planked Trout
with Fennel, Bacon & Orange

It's been my culinary dream to eat fly-fished trout cooked in a cast iron skillet over a campfire. When the opportunity comes, I'll have the ingredients to make this version stuffed with bacon, orange, and fennel. (I just haven't worked out who's going to carry the cast iron skillet!)

alder
WOOD PELLETS

**450°F (232°C);
300°F (149°C)**
GRILL TEMP

30 to 40 mins
COOK TIME

Serves **4** • Prep time **20 mins** • Rest time **none**

4 whole trout, each about 14 to 16oz (400 to 450g), cleaned and gutted, fins removed

coarse salt

freshly ground black pepper

for the filling

1 large navel orange

4 slices of thick-cut bacon, diced

1 large fennel bulb, trimmed, halved, decored, and diced, green fronds reserved

4oz (110g) baby spinach, about 6 cups

coarse salt

freshly ground black pepper

1. Preheat the grill to 450°F (232°C). Place 4 cedar planks on the grate and allow them to singe slightly on both sides. Remove them from the grill and place them on a heatproof surface to cool.

2. Lower the temperature to 300°F (149°C).

3. Slice 4 thin rounds from the center of the orange and then slice each in half for 8 pieces total. Zest the remainder of the orange and set aside.

4. In a cold skillet on the stovetop over medium heat, sauté the bacon, until the fat has rendered and the bacon is golden brown, about 6 to 8 minutes, stirring frequently. Use a slotted spoon to transfer the bacon to paper towels to drain. Add the fennel to the fat in the skillet and cook until tender crisp, about 5 minutes. Add the spinach and stir until it wilts, about 1 to 2 minutes. Squeeze the juice of one of the reserved orange ends over the mixture. Add the drained bacon. Season with salt and pepper and then stir. Remove the skillet from the stovetop and set aside.

5. Rinse each trout inside and out under cold running water and pat dry with paper towels. Place three 12-inch (30.5cm) pieces of butcher's twine on each plank and place a trout on top. Season the inside of each fish with salt and pepper. Place two half-rounds of orange in each belly, rind side facing out. Top with some of the filling. Tie the trout with the butcher's twine and trim any ends. Repeat with the remaining trout.

6. Place the planks on the grate and cook the trout until they're cooked through, about 30 to 40 minutes.

7. Remove the planks from the grill and remove the twine. Top each trout with a few curls of orange zest and some reserved fennel fronds. Serve the trout on the planks.

Nutrition per 1 trout

Calories **646** • Total fat **26g** • Carbs **13g** • Dietary fiber **4g** • Sugars **4g** • Protein **84g**

Prosciutto-Wrapped Scallops

Scallops wrapped with bacon are menu staples at some restaurants. But scallops and bacon have different cooking times, meaning the scallops are woefully overcooked by the time the bacon crisps. Wrap the scallops in prosciutto and the problem is solved.

cherry or apple
WOOD PELLETS

450°F (232°C)
GRILL TEMP

6 to 10 mins
COOK TIME

Serves **4** • Prep time **15 mins** • Rest time **none**

1½lb (680g) jumbo sea or diver scallops (size U-10)

8 to 10 thin slices of prosciutto, each halved lengthwise

coarse salt

freshly ground black pepper

for the butter

8oz (225g) unsalted butter

2 tsp minced fresh curly or flat-leaf parsley

1½ tsp finely grated orange zest

1 tbsp freshly squeezed orange juice

1 tsp finely grated lemon zest

1 tsp finely grated lime zest

½ tsp coarse salt

1. Preheat the grill to 450°F (232°C).

2. In a small saucepan on the stovetop over medium-low heat, make the citrus butter by melting the butter. Add the remaining ingredients and simmer for 3 to 5 minutes to blend the flavors. Keep warm.

3. Rinse the scallops under cold running water and dry with paper towels. Place each scallop on its side at the end of a piece of prosciutto and wrap the prosciutto around the scallop. Secure with a toothpick. Season the exposed sides of the scallop with salt and pepper.

4. Place the scallops exposed sides down on the grate and grill until the edges of the prosciutto begin to frizzle and the scallop is warm inside, about 3 to 5 minutes per side.

5. Transfer the scallops to a platter. Brush with some of the warm citrus butter before serving. Serve the remaining butter on the side.

TIPS | *Be sure to buy dry-packed scallops. Avoid scallops that have been soaked in tripolyphosphate, a chemical that whitens scallops and adds as much as 30% to their weight. For an attractive presentation, thread the prosciutto-wrapped scallops on bamboo skewers before grilling, 3 or 4 scallops per skewer. Brush with the butter before serving.*

Nutrition per 3 scallops

Calories **605** • Total fat **50g** • Carbs **5g** • Dietary fiber **0g** • Sugars **0g** • Protein **35g**

Moules Marinières
with Garlic Butter Sauce

An Irishman shipwrecked on the coast of Normandy in the 13th century is credited with developing the recipe for "sailor's mussels." He and his crew resourcefully harvested the mussels clinging to their nets and used local ingredients to cook them over wood fires.

alder
WOOD PELLETS

450°F (232°C)
GRILL TEMP

10 to 12 mins
COOK TIME

Serves **4** • Prep time **15 mins** • Rest time **none**

3lb (1.4kg) fresh mussels, scrubbed under cold running water and debearded

lemon wedges

crusty bread (optional)

for the sauce

6 tbsp unsalted butter

3 garlic cloves, peeled and minced

1 cup dry white wine or hard cider

1 tbsp freshly squeezed lemon juice

2 tsp hot sauce, plus more

coarse salt

freshly ground black pepper

2 tbsp chopped fresh curly parsley or tarragon

1. Preheat the grill to 450°F (232°C).

2. In a small saucepan on the stovetop over medium-low heat, make the sauce by melting the butter. Add the garlic and sauté for 1 to 2 minutes. Add the wine, lemon juice, and hot sauce. Season with salt and pepper to taste. Simmer for 5 minutes. Remove the saucepan from the heat and stir in the parsley. Keep warm.

3. Discard any mussels that are cracked or don't snap shut when tapped. Place the mussels in a large aluminum foil roasting pan and cover tightly with heavy-duty aluminum foil.

4. Place the pan on the grate and steam the mussels until the shells open, about 10 to 12 minutes. Remove the pan from the grill and use long-handled tongs to remove the foil from the pan. (Be careful of escaping steam.) Use the tongs to discard any mussels that don't open.

5. Pour the reserved garlic butter sauce over the mussels. Serve from the pan or transfer the mussels to a shallow serving bowl. Serve immediately with lemon wedges, additional hot sauce, and crusty bread (if using) to sop up the juices.

TIPS | *Instead of a foil pan, you can use a large grill basket or a perforated tray (uncovered). The mussels will pick up more smoke, but you'll lose the juices. Advise guests to use a set of mussel shells like miniature tongs to pluck and eat the remaining mussels.*

Nutrition per 15 mussels

Calories **365** • Total fat **11g** • Carbs **14g** • Dietary fiber **0g** • Sugars **0g** • Protein **41g**

Smoke-Roasted Halibut
with Mixed Herb Vinaigrette

alder
WOOD PELLETS

400°F (204°C)
GRILL TEMP

8 to 12 mins
COOK TIME

Referred to by fisherman as "the prime rib of the sea," halibut will delight any seafood lover with its sweet taste and firm but tender texture. Like prime rib, this largest of the Pacific flatfish is pricey because of strictly enforced quotas. But the expense is well worth the dining experience.

Serves **4** • Prep time **10 mins** • Rest time **none**

4 halibut fillets, each about 6 to 8oz (170 to 225g)

for the vinaigrette
2 tbsp white wine vinegar or sherry vinegar, plus more

¼ tsp coarse salt, plus more

¼ tsp freshly ground black pepper, plus more

½ cup extra virgin olive oil

2 tbsp minced fresh herbs, such as dill, flat-leaf parsley, or oregano

for serving
4 cups loosely packed baby arugula, spinach, or other mixed greens

1 lemon, cut lengthwise into 4 wedges

1. Preheat the grill to 400°F (204°C).

2. In a small bowl, make the vinaigrette by whisking together the vinegar, and salt and pepper. Whisk until the salt dissolves. Continue to whisk while slowly adding the olive oil. Whisk until the vinaigrette is emulsified. Stir in the herbs. Taste, adding vinegar or salt and pepper to taste. Pour ⅓ of the vinaigrette into a separate container. Reserve the remainder.

3. Place the fillets on a rimmed sheet pan. Lightly brush both sides with the smaller portion of vinaigrette. (Dividing the vinaigrette into two containers prevents cross-contamination.) Lightly season with salt and pepper.

4. Place the fillets on the grate at an angle to the bars. Grill until the edges begin to look opaque, about 4 to 6 minutes. Gently turn and grill until the fish is cooked through, about 4 to 6 minutes more. (A fillet will break into clean flakes when pressed with a fork when it's done.)

5. Remove the fish from the grill. Place the greens in a large bowl and toss them with 2 to 3 tablespoons of the reserved vinaigrette (you want the greens lightly coated) and divide between 4 plates. Place a fillet on the greens on each plate. Drizzle a bit more of the vinaigrette over the top. Serve with lemon wedges.

Nutrition per 1 fillet
Calories **400** • Total fat **29g** • Carbs **2g** • Dietary fiber **1g** • Sugars **1g** • Protein **36g**

Grilled Salmon Steaks
with Dill Sauce

Salmon has been called one of the most nutritious foods on the planet, with its payload of omega-3 fatty acids, B vitamins, and potassium. If you can find it (and afford it), buy wild-caught salmon from the Pacific. Grilled quickly, it's the perfect entrée for a busy weeknight.

alder
WOOD PELLETS

450°F (232°C)
GRILL TEMP

8 mins
COOK TIME

Serves **4** • Prep time **10 mins** • Rest time **None**

4 salmon steaks, each about 6 to 8oz (170 to 225g) and 1 inch (2.5cm) thick

extra virgin olive oil

coarse salt

freshly ground rainbow peppercorns or freshly ground black pepper

lemon wedges

for the sauce

1 cup reduced-fat mayo

⅓ cup light sour cream

¼ cup chopped fresh dill

2 tbsp freshly squeezed lemon juice

coarse salt

freshly ground black pepper

sprigs of fresh dill

1. Preheat the grill to 450°F (232°C)

2. In a small bowl, make the dill sauce by combining the mayo, sour cream, dill, and lemon juice. Mix until smooth. Season with salt and pepper to taste. Transfer to a serving bowl. Scatter the dill sprigs over the top. Cover and refrigerate until ready to serve.

3. Brush the salmon with olive oil and season with salt and pepper. Place the salmon on the grate at an angle to the bars. Grill until grill marks begin to appear, about 4 minutes. Use a thin-bladed spatula to turn the salmon. Grill until the internal temperature reaches 140°F (60°C), about 4 minutes more.

4. Transfer the salmon to a platter. Serve immediately with the lemon wedges and dill sauce.

TIPS | *Rainbow peppercorns are a mix of colored peppercorns: pink, green, white, and black. They can be found in the spice aisles of most supermarkets. Accompany the salmon with* **Grilled Fennel** *(page 170) or* **Prosciutto-Wrapped Asparagus** *(page 171).*

Nutrition per 1 salmon steak

Calories **607** • Total fat **50g** • Carbs **1g** • Dietary fiber **0g** • Sugars **1g** • Protein **35g**

Mexican Mahi Mahi
with Baja Cabbage Slaw

The Baja Peninsula is well known to surfers and foodies alike—its epic waves and battered fried fish attracting both groups in droves. You don't need to hang 10 to recreate the flavors of Ensenada's beach community. Why mask the flavors of pristine white fish when you can grill it?

hickory or oak
WOOD PELLETS

450°F (232°C)
GRILL TEMP

8 to 10 mins
COOK TIME

Serves **4** • Prep time **10 mins** • Rest time **none**

1½lb (680g) skinless mahi mahi, cod, or other firm white fish fillets

coarse salt

freshly ground black pepper

chili powder

lime wedges

for the slaw

2 cups finely shredded green cabbage

2 cups finely shredded purple cabbage

4 tbsp reduced-fat mayo

2 tsp hot sauce, plus more

2 tsp freshly squeezed lime juice

½ tsp coarse salt

for the marinade

¼ cup freshly squeezed orange juice

¼ cup freshly squeezed lime juice

2 tbsp extra virgin olive oil

1. In a medium bowl, make the slaw by combining the ingredients. Stir well. Transfer to a serving bowl. Cover and refrigerate until ready to serve.

2. Place the fish fillets in a baking dish and pour the orange and lime juices and olive oil over them. Turn the fillets to coat thoroughly. Cover and refrigerate for 15 to 20 minutes.

3. Preheat the grill to 450°F (232°C).

4. Drain the fish and pat dry with paper towels. (Discard the marinade.) Season the fillets on both sides with salt and pepper and chili powder. Place the fillets on the grate and grill until golden brown, about 4 to 5 minutes per side, turning with a thin-bladed spatula.

5. Transfer the fish to a platter. Serve with the slaw and lime wedges.

TIPS | *You can also serve the mahi mahi with pico de gallo, pickled red onions, avocados, fresh cilantro leaves, sliced radishes, Mexican crema or light sour cream, and crumbled queso fresca or cotija cheese.*

Nutrition per 6oz (170g)

Calories **331** • Total fat **10g** • Carbs **11g** • Dietary fiber **3g** • Sugars **4g** • Protein **48g**

Mezcal Shrimp
with Salsa de Molcajete

If you're unfamiliar with mezcal, it's a distilled spirit from Mexico. It's made just as it was 200 years ago: agave hearts are roasted in underground pits before being mashed and fermented. It has a smoky taste, echoing flavors the shrimp pick up from grilling with wood smoke.

mesquite
WOOD PELLETS

450°F (232°C)
GRILL TEMP

10 to 14 mins
COOK TIME

Serves **4** • Prep time **10 mins** • Rest time **5 mins**

18 to 24 jumbo shrimp, about 1½lb (680g) total, peeled and deveined

⅓ cup mezcal

juice of ½ lime

2 tbsp extra virgin olive oil

2 tsp coarse salt

1 tsp ground cumin

lime wedges

for the salsa

2 Roma tomatoes

2 tomatillos, husked and washed

2 garlic cloves, peeled and impaled on a toothpick

1 jalapeño or serrano pepper

1 small white onion, halved

½ tsp coarse salt, plus more

juice of ½ lime

¼ cup loosely packed fresh cilantro leaves

1. Preheat the grill to 450°F (232°C).

2. In a large bowl, combine the shrimp, mezcal, lime juice, olive oil, salt, and ground cumin. Toss with your hands to mix thoroughly. Set aside for 15 minutes and then toss once more.

3. Begin to make the salsa by placing the tomatoes, tomatillos, garlic, jalapeño, and onion on the grate. Grill until they begin to char, about 3 minutes for the garlic and about 6 to 8 minutes for the other vegetables, turning as needed. Transfer the vegetables to a rimmed sheet pan. Remove the skewers from the garlic. Let everything cool. Coarsely chop the vegetables and leave them in separate piles.

4. Place the garlic in the molcajete and add the salt. Mash the garlic to a purée using the temolote. Add the onion and grind it into the garlic paste. Stir in the jalapeño (deseeded for a milder salsa), tomatoes, and tomatillos. Stir in the lime juice and cilantro leaves. Taste, adding salt. (If you don't own a molcajete or temolote, prepare the salsa using a small food processor.)

5. Drain the shrimp and discard the marinade. Thread the shrimp on wood or bamboo skewers. Place the shrimp on the grate and grill until they're white and opaque, about 4 to 6 minutes, tossing with tongs.

6. Transfer the shrimp to a platter. Serve with the salsa and lime wedges.

Nutrition per 6 shrimp

Calories **346** • Total fat **10g** • Carbs **12g** • Dietary fiber **2g** • Sugars **4g** • Protein **40g**

SOUPS
& SALADS

Roasted Red Pepper & Mozzarella Salad

hickory
WOOD PELLETS

450°F (232°C)
GRILL TEMP

8 to 10 mins
COOK TIME

I've been making this visually stunning salad for years—and it never fails to elicit compliments or requests for seconds. You can make it your own by substituting capers or caperberries for the olives or replacing the mozzarella with crumbled feta, goat cheese, or grated Manchego.

Serves **4** • Prep time **20 mins** • Rest time **10 mins**

4 bell peppers (mixed colors), destemmed, halved, and deseeded

½ small red onion (cut through the stem end), thinly sliced crosswise

12 brined and pitted olives, such as Cerignola or Kalamata, coarsely chopped

3oz (85g) fresh mozzarella pearls or cubes

small fresh basil leaves

for the vinaigrette

2 tbsp red wine vinegar or sherry vinegar

1 tbsp chopped fresh basil

1 garlic clove, peeled and minced

½ tsp coarse salt

½ tsp freshly ground black pepper

⅓ cup extra virgin olive oil

1. Preheat the grill to 450°F (232°C).

2. In a jar with a tight-fitting lid, make the vinaigrette by combining the red wine vinegar, basil, garlic, and salt and pepper. Shake vigorously to dissolve the salt. Add the olive oil and shake again until the mixture is emulsified. Set aside.

3. Place the pepper halves skin side down on the grate and roast until the skin blisters and blackens, about 8 to 10 minutes. (You want to leave the peppers somewhat raw on the inside.)

4. Transfer the peppers to a rimmed baking sheet and let cool until they can be handled comfortably. Peel off the skin with your fingers or a paring knife. Don't worry if you don't get all of it—a few blackened bits are okay.

5. Slice each pepper half lengthwise into quarters and place attractively on a platter, alternating colors. Scatter the onion slices, olives, and mozzarella among the peppers. Shake the vinaigrette again if it has begun to separate and drizzle evenly over the salad. Scatter the basil over the top. Serve at room temperature.

TIPS | *Years ago, a cooking teacher from Emilia-Romagna told me to always look for bell peppers that have four lobes on the bottom. They are females, she said, and are sweeter than the three-lobed males. True? I'm not sure. What I do know is that red, yellow, and orange peppers are much sweeter than their green counterparts—almost like fruit.*

Nutrition per ¼ salad

Calories **243** • Total fat **23g** • Carbs **7g** • Dietary fiber **3g** • Sugars **3g** • Protein **6g**

Steak Salad
with Ginger & Miso Dressing

This is a wonderful go-to meal when you don't want to heat up the kitchen or feel like a light lunch or supper. Many of the ingredients can be picked up at your supermarket's salad bar. Oftentimes, flank steak or top sirloin are labeled as "London broil" at the meat counter.

cherry or apple
WOOD PELLETS

450°F (232°C)
GRILL TEMP

8 to 10 mins
COOK TIME

Serves **4** • Prep time **20 mins** • Rest time **5 mins**

1½lb (680g) flank steak or top sirloin

coarse salt

freshly ground black pepper

½ cup salted cashews or peanuts, roughly chopped (optional)

Ginger & Miso Dressing (page 25)

for the salad

12oz (340g) mixed salad greens

3 scallions, trimmed, white and green parts thinly sliced on a sharp diagonal

½ hothouse cucumber, thinly sliced

1 carrot, trimmed, peeled, and shredded

1 cup shelled edamame

1 cup cherry tomatoes, halved

¼ cup loosely packed fresh cilantro leaves

¼ cup loosely packed fresh basil leaves, preferably Thai, or fresh mint

1. Preheat the grill to 450°F (232°C).

2. Season the steak on both sides with salt and pepper. Place the steak on the grate and grill until the internal temperature reaches 130°F (54°C), about 4 to 5 minutes per side.

3. Transfer the steak to a cutting board and let rest for 5 minutes. Thinly slice against the grain on a diagonal.

4. Place the greens on a platter with a deep well. Top with the scallions, cucumber, carrot, edamame, tomatoes, cilantro, and basil. Place the sliced steak on the salad. Drizzle the dressing over the top. Scatter the cashews (if using) over the top before serving.

TIPS | *Thai basil has a purple stem and a spicy, anise-y flavor that differentiates it from the more common Italian basil. Find it at well-stocked supermarkets or Asian groceries. Also, it's very easy to grow. If you can't find it, substitute fresh Italian basil and/or mint. Miso can often be found refrigerated, although shelf-stable brands are also available.*

Nutrition per ¼ salad

Calories **667** • Total fat **45g** • Carbs **21g** • Dietary fiber **5g** • Sugars **4g** • Protein **47g**

Mexican Corn Salad

If you've ever eaten Mexican street corn (*elote*), you'll see its influence on this summery salad. In addition to grilled corn, mayo, lime juice, chili powder, and crumbled cheese, it has grilled poblano and bell peppers, hot sauce, and fresh cilantro. Make when sweet corn is at its peak.

mesquite
WOOD PELLETS

450°F (232°C)
GRILL TEMP

8 to 12 mins
COOK TIME

Serves **6** • Prep time **10 mins** • Rest time **none**

6 ears of sweet corn, shucked and silk removed

6 scallions, trimmed

2 poblano peppers

1 red bell pepper

for the dressing
½ cup reduced-fat mayo, plus more

¼ cup light sour cream

juice of 1 lime

zest of ½ lime

2 tsp chili powder

2 tsp hot sauce, plus more

coarse salt

freshly ground black pepper

for the salad
2 heads of lettuce, leaves separated, washed, and dried

1 cup crumbled cotija, queso fresco, feta, or grated Parmigiano-Reggiano cheese

½ cup loosely packed fresh cilantro

baby heirloom or cherry tomatoes (optional)

1. Preheat the grill to 450°F (232°C).

2. Place the corn, scallions, and peppers on the grate. Grill the scallions until softened, about 3 to 4 minutes, turning as needed. Grill the corn and peppers until the corn has browned patches and the skins on the poblanos and bell pepper have blistered and charred, about 8 to 12 minutes, turning as needed. Transfer the vegetables to a rimmed baking sheet to cool.

3. Stand each ear of corn on its broad end on a cutting board. Use smooth downward strokes of a knife to cut off the kernels. Transfer them to a large bowl. (Discard the cobs or save them to make vegetable stock.) Peel the charred skin off the peppers and then destem and deseed them. Dice the peppers and add them to the corn. Thinly slice the scallions and add them to the bowl.

4. In a small bowl, make the dressing by whisking together the mayo, sour cream, lime juice and zest, chili powder, and hot sauce. Season with salt and pepper to taste. Add the dressing to the corn mixture and stir gently with a rubber spatula to combine.

5. Place the lettuce leaves on 6 individual plates, with their ends pointed toward the center. Top each with an equal amount of corn salad (about ½ to ¾ cup), cheese, and cilantro leaves. Add 2 to 3 tomatoes on the side (if using). Serve with additional hot sauce.

Nutrition per ¾ cup
Calories **309** • Total fat **21g** • Carbs **24g** • Dietary fiber **4g** • Sugars **6g** • Protein **10g**

Smoked Gazpacho Caprese

oak or pecan
WOOD PELLETS

200°F (93°C)
GRILL TEMP

20 mins
COOK TIME

My Andalusian colleagues would be disappointed to learn I've been tinkering with one of their classic cold soups: gazpacho. Smoking it. Adding Italian touches, like basil and mozzarella. Punishable offenses, all. But the result is very good—and refreshing on a hot day.

Serves **4** • Prep time **15 mins** • Rest time **none**

2lb (1kg) vine-ripened tomatoes, destemmed, decored, and coarsely chopped

1 small white onion, peeled and coarsely chopped

1 bell pepper, preferably red, orange, or yellow, destemmed, deseeded, and coarsely chopped

½ hothouse cucumber, coarsely chopped

2 garlic cloves, peeled and coarsely chopped

1 thick slice of country-style bread, crust removed and bread torn into several pieces

5 large fresh basil leaves, torn or coarsely chopped, plus 4 small leaves

2 tbsp sherry vinegar or red wine vinegar, plus more

½ tsp ground cumin

coarse salt

freshly ground black pepper

¼ cup extra virgin olive oil, plus more

4oz (110g) fresh mozzarella ciliegine, mozzarella pearls, or diced fresh mozzarella

1. Preheat the grill to 200°F (93°C).

2. On a rimmed sheet pan, combine the tomatoes, onion, bell pepper, cucumber, garlic, and bread. Place the pan on the grate and smoke the vegetables and bread for 20 minutes, stirring once or twice. (You want the vegetables to remain raw.) Remove the pan from the grill and let the mixture cool.

3. Place the mixture into a blender. Add the torn basil leaves, sherry, and cumin. Season with salt and pepper to taste. Pulse the machine a few times and purée until smooth. With the machine running, slowly add the olive oil. Taste the gazpacho, adding more sherry vinegar, salt, or pepper. Transfer the gazpacho to a glass pitcher, cover, and chill.

4. Pour the gazpacho into 4 bowls, cups, or glasses. Scatter the mozzarella and drizzle the olive oil over the top. Add a small basil leaf to each serving.

TIPS | *If the gazpacho seems too thick, add ice water 1 tablespoon at a time until the desired consistency is reached. The soup can easily be turned into an appetizer by serving it in shot glasses—known as "gazpacho shooters."*

Nutrition per 1 cup
Calories **264** • Total fat **18g** • Carbs **17g** • Dietary fiber **4g** • Sugars **7g** • Protein **11g**

Pork Belly Salad

Grilled salad? Absolutely. I got the idea from my friend, grilling and barbecue expert Steven Raichlen, who's been spreading the gospel for years about grilled Caesar salads. This one features a smoked pork belly spiced with mustard powder and Chinese five-spice powder.

hickory or apple
WOOD PELLETS

450°F (232°C)
GRILL TEMP

7 to 10 mins
COOK TIME

Serves **8** • Prep time **15 mins** • Rest time **none**

1lb (450g) **Spiced Pork Belly** (page 86)

for the salad
8 unblemished romaine hearts, halved lengthwise

extra virgin olive oil

2 scallions, trimmed, white and green parts thinly sliced crosswise

1 cup halved cherry tomatoes (red, yellow, or a mix)

for the dressing
2 garlic cloves, peeled and coarsely chopped

⅓ cup extra virgin olive oil

⅓ cup reduced-fat mayo

2 tbsp freshly squeezed lemon juice, plus more

1½ tbsp Dijon mustard

2 tsp honey

2 tsp Worcestershire sauce

½ tsp coarse salt, plus more

½ tsp freshly ground black pepper, plus more

1. Preheat the grill to 450°F (232°C).

2. In a blender, make the dressing by combining the ingredients. Purée until smooth and creamy. Taste, adding more salt, pepper, and lemon juice if needed. Set aside. (Cover and refrigerate if not using within 1 hour.)

3. Lightly brush the cut sides of the romaine hearts with olive oil. Place the hearts cut sides down on the grate and grill until the lettuce has picked up some smoke and grill marks but remains raw, about 1 to 2 minutes. Transfer the lettuce to a cutting board and coarsely chop. (Leave the grill going.) Place the lettuce, scallions, and tomatoes in a salad bowl. Set aside.

4. Cut the pork belly into ¾-inch (2cm) cubes and place them in a grill basket. Place the basket on the grate and grill the pork until crispy and brown, about 6 to 8 minutes, stirring often.

5. Remove the basket from the grill and let the pork cool slightly. Add the pork to the salad bowl. Drizzle the salad with half the dressing and toss to coat. Add more dressing if needed. Serve immediately.

TIPS | *The heavier ingredients, such as the pork belly and tomatoes, will gravitate toward the bottom of the salad bowl. Make sure everyone receives a relatively equal portion of the ingredients.*

Nutrition per ⅛ salad
Calories **695** • Total fat **75g** • Carbs **14g** • Dietary fiber **3g** • Sugars **3g** • Protein **13g**

Smoked Trout Salad
with Endive Scoops

alder
WOOD PELLETS

150°F (66°C);
225°F (107°C)
GRILL TEMP

2 to 3 hrs
COOK TIME

Years ago, I worked in an office that was a 5-minute walk from one of New York City's iconic delis—one known for its smoked fish, which explains how I got hooked on smoked fish salad. But you can make a superior version from start to finish by using your pellet smoker.

Serves **4 to 6** • Prep time **15 mins** • Rest time **30 mins**

3 trout, cleaned and gutted, each about 12oz (340g)

for the brine
2 quarts (2 liters) distilled water
½ cup coarse salt
¼ cup light brown sugar or low-carb substitute

for the salad
1 celery rib, diced
⅓ cup diced red onion
1 tbsp freshly squeezed lemon juice
½ cup reduced-fat mayo, plus more
coarse salt
freshly ground black pepper
2 large heads of Belgian endive or Treviso

1. In a saucepan on the stovetop over medium-high heat, make the brine by bringing the ingredients to a boil. Remove the pan from the heat and let the brine cool to room temperature. Cover and refrigerate until cool.

2. Submerge the trout in the brine. If they float, place a resealable bag of ice on top. Refrigerate for 4 hours.

3. Place a wire rack over a rimmed sheet pan. Remove the trout from the brine. (Discard the brine.) Rinse the trout under cold running water and pat dry with paper towels. Place the trout on the wire rack. Prop the cavities of the fish open with toothpicks to encourage good smoke circulation. Place the pan in a cool area with good air circulation—such as near a fan. In 2 to 4 hours, you'll notice the trout has developed a pellicle—a kind of sticky skin or coating that will help the smoke adhere to the fish. (Don't skip this step.)

4. Preheat the grill to 150°F (66°C).

5. Place the trout on the grate and smoke until the fish flakes easily when pressed with a fork and the internal temperature reaches 140°F (60°C), about 2 to 3 hours.

6. Remove the trout from the grill and let cool to room temperature. Remove the toothpicks. Skin and debone the trout. Break the meat into flakes. In a large bowl, combine the trout, celery, onion, lemon juice, and mayo. Season with salt and pepper to taste. Add more mayo 1 tablespoon at a time if needed.

7. Transfer the salad to a serving bowl. Cover and refrigerate before serving with endive leaves.

TIPS | *Belgian endive is a member of the chicory family and consists of a tight bundle of white to pale green leaves attached to a central core. Treviso (a form of radicchio) is identified by its wine-colored leaves. Together, the two look beautiful on a plate.*

Nutrition per ½ cup
Calories **261** • Total fat **12g** • Carbs **10g** • Dietary fiber **8g** • Sugars **2g** • Protein **28g**

Lobster Salad Lettuce Cups

A lobsterman from Maine once told me the key to great lobster salad is to keep it simple. I'm not sure he'd approve of the scallion, but I like the way it tastes. Ditto for the wood smoke. Personally, I find tails easier to work with. But you can certainly make this salad using whole lobsters.

apple or cherry
WOOD PELLETS

300°F (149°C)
GRILL TEMP

30 to 35 mins
COOK TIME

Serves **4** • Prep time **20 mins** • Rest time **none**

4 cold-water lobster tails, each about 5 to 6oz (140 to 170g), thawed if frozen

4 tbsp unsalted butter, melted

coarse salt

freshly ground black pepper

⅓ to ½ cup reduced-fat mayo

⅓ cup finely diced celery, preferably from the pale, inner stalks

1 scallion, trimmed, white and green parts thinly sliced

2 tsp freshly squeezed lemon juice

butter lettuce or radicchio leaves (or a mix), washed, dried, and chilled

1. Preheat the grill to 300°F (149°C).

2. Use kitchen shears or a heavy chef's knife to cut cleanly through the back of each lobster shell toward the tail. Loosen the meat from the shell. Gently coax the meat away from the shell, leaving it attached at the tail. Lift the meat on top of the shell. Devein if necessary. Brush the tail meat with butter and season with salt and pepper.

3. Place the tails on the grate and smoke until the meat is firm and opaque and the internal temperature reaches 140°F (60°C), about 30 to 35 minutes. (Don't overcook the lobster tails.)

4. Remove the tails from the grill and let cool. Remove the meat from the shells. You should have about ¾ of a pound (340g).

5. In a medium bowl, combine the mayo, celery, scallion, and lemon juice. Season with salt and black pepper to taste. Dice the lobster meat and add to the bowl. Gently stir to combine. (Cover and chill if desired.)

6. Place one or two lettuce or radicchio leaves on a plate and spoon some of the lobster salad into them. Serve immediately.

TIPS | *Tin snips work well for cutting lobster shells. I keep a clean pair in my kitchen that I use only for food. You can freeze the shells to use for lobster stock.*

Nutrition per 6oz (170g)
Calories **351** • Total fat **27g** • Carbs **3g** • Dietary fiber **1g** • Sugars **1g** • Protein **25g**

Grilled Cantaloupe
with Halloumi & Prosciutto

apple
WOOD PELLETS

450°F (232°C)
GRILL TEMP

13 to 18 mins
COOK TIME

Have you ever attended a party where most guests were unknown to each other but got along famously? That describes this salad. It's a mix of disparate elements—grilled sweet cantaloupe; shards of crisped salty prosciutto; and a unique grilling cheese from Cyprus called halloumi.

Serves **4 to 6** • Prep time **10 mins** • Rest time **none**

1 large cantaloupe, halved, deseeded, and cut into 8 wedges, rind removed

8oz (225g) halloumi, drained and sliced into 8 slabs

extra virgin olive oil

4oz (110g) thinly sliced prosciutto

fresh basil leaves

extra virgin olive oil (optional)

crunchy sea salt

freshly ground black pepper (optional)

1. Place a cast iron skillet on the grate. Preheat the grill to 450°F (232°C).

2. Brush the cantaloupe and halloumi on both sides with olive oil. Place the cantaloupe cut side down and cheese on the grate. Grill the cheese for 1 to 2 minutes. Turn and grill for 3 to 4 minutes more. Grill the melon until grill marks appear, about 3 to 4 minutes per side.

3. Place the prosciutto in the skillet and cook until crisp, about 3 to 4 minutes, moving it around as needed. Transfer the cheese, melon, and prosciutto to a platter.

4. Place the melon and cheese attractively on the platter. Drizzle with olive oil. Crumble the frizzled prosciutto over the top. Scatter the basil around the platter. Serve with olive oil (if using) and salt and pepper (if using).

Nutrition per 2 melon wedges, 2oz (55g) cheese, and 2 prosciutto slices

Calories **335** • Total fat **20g** • Carbs **19g** • Dietary fiber **2g** • Sugars **16g** • Protein **22g**

Lone Star Chili

This recipe came from a friend who interviewed a great-granddaughter of one of San Antonio's "Chili Queens." They were Hispanic women who sold their version of chili con carne on Military Plaza from the 1860s to the 1930s. By the way, Texans prefer their chili without beans

mesquite
WOOD PELLETS

225°F (107°C)
GRILL TEMP

1½ to 2 hrs
COOK TIME

Serves **8** • Prep time **1 hr** • Rest time **none**

4 or 5 dried guajillo chilis, destemmed and deseeded

3 dried ancho chilis, destemmed and deseeded

2 tbsp lard or vegetable oil

2lb (1kg) beef chuck, cut into ¾-inch (2cm) cubes

1lb (450g) boneless pork ribs, cut into ¾-inch (2cm) cubes

1 medium white onion, peeled and diced

2 fresh Anaheim or poblano peppers, destemmed, deseeded, and diced

4 garlic cloves, peeled and minced

¼ cup chili powder, plus more

2 tbsp light brown sugar or low-carb substitute

2 tbsp corn masa or all-purpose flour

1½ tsp ground cumin

1½ tsp dried Mexican oregano

1½ tsp coarse salt

1½ tsp freshly ground black pepper

4 cups beef broth, plus more

½ cup low-carb beer

½ cup Mexican-style tomato sauce

1. In a cast iron Dutch oven on the stovetop over medium heat, toast the guajillo and ancho chilis until they're fragrant, about 3 minutes, stirring frequently. (Don't let them scorch or they'll be bitter.) Transfer the chilis to a heatproof bowl and cover with boiling water. Let them soak for 30 minutes. When the chilis are soft, add them and half the soaking liquid to a blender or food processor. Purée until smooth. Set aside.

2. Preheat the grill to 225°F (107°C).

3. In the same Dutch oven on the stovetop over medium-high heat, melt the lard. Sear the beef and pork in batches until well browned on all sides, about 4 to 6 minutes for each batch, stirring frequently. (Don't overcrowd the pot.) Transfer the browned meat to a heatproof bowl and set aside.

4. Add the onion, peppers, and garlic to the Dutch oven and sauté until the vegetables have softened, about 5 minutes. Return the meat and any accumulated juices to the pot and stir in the chili powder, brown sugar, corn masa, cumin, oregano, and salt and pepper. Stir and cook for 2 to 3 minutes. Stir in the beef broth, beer, and tomato sauce.

5. Place the Dutch oven on the grate. Leave the lid off the Dutch oven, but close the grill lid. Smoke the chili until the meat is fall-apart tender, about 1½ to 2 hours, stirring occasionally. If the chili seems too thick, add a bit more beef broth.

6. Remove the Dutch oven from the grill and ladle the chili into bowls, cups, or mugs. Top with grated Cheddar cheese, light sour cream, and thinly sliced scallions before serving.

Nutrition per 1½ cups

Calories **1046** • Total fat **78g** • Carbs **6g** • Dietary fiber **1g** • Sugars **4g** • Protein **75g**

Greek Gyro Salad

oak
WOOD PELLETS

325°F (163°C)
GRILL TEMP

30 to 45 mins
COOK TIME

You've likely been advised not to overwork ground meats when making burgers and meatloaf. But surprisingly, overworking is the key to successfully making gyro meat. You want the mixture to be almost sticky before shaping it into a loaf, which you'll grill to add to a salad.

Serves **4** • Prep time **45 mins** • Rest time **30 mins**

½ medium red onion, peeled

2 tsp coarse salt, divided

4 garlic cloves, peeled and finely minced

1lb (450g) ground beef

1lb (450g) ground lamb or pork

1½ tsp dried Greek oregano

1½ tsp dried marjoram

1½ tsp dried rosemary

1 tsp freshly ground black pepper

extra virgin olive oil

for the salad

6 cups mixed salad greens, chilled

4 Roma tomatoes, sliced crosswise or cut into wedges

1 hothouse cucumber, thinly sliced

½ medium red onion, peeled and thinly sliced

½ cup brined and pitted Kalamata olives, drained

1 cup crumbled feta cheese

Tzatziki (page 69)

pita bread or flatbread wedges (optional)

1. Grate the onion over a sieve. Add 1 teaspoon of salt and let the onion drain for 10 minutes. Press on the onion to extract the remaining juice. Place the onion and garlic in the bowl of a stand mixer. Add the beef, lamb, oregano, marjoram, rosemary, black pepper, and the remaining 1 teaspoon of salt. Use the paddle attachment on medium speed to thoroughly mix the ingredients until they become tacky, about 5 minutes.

2. Coat a loaf pan with olive oil. Wet your hands with cold water and firmly press the meat mixture into the prepared pan. (Use the bottom of a second loaf pan to press on the first to eliminate any air holes and to flatten the top.) Cover the pan with aluminum foil and refrigerate for 2 to 4 hours.

3. Preheat the grill to 325°F (163°C).

4. Place the loaf pan on the grate and smoke the meat for 1 hour. Carefully pour off any accumulated fat directly into your drip bucket or another container. Place the meat on the grate and grill until the internal temperature reaches 160°F (40°C), about 30 to 45 minutes.

5. Remove the loaf from the grill and wrap the meat in aluminum foil. Place the loaf in a clean loaf pan and place something heavy on top of the meat, such as a foil-covered brick or canned goods. Let the meat cool for 30 minutes. Refrigerate for several hours or overnight.

6. Unwrap the loaf. Use a sharp knife to slice the meat into thin slices, each no thicker than ¼ inch (.5cm).

7. Place the greens on a platter with a deep well. Place the tomatoes, cucumber, red onion, olives, and gyro slices on the greens. Scatter the feta over the top. Serve with tzatziki and pita bread (if using).

Nutrition per ¼ salad

Calories **880** • Total fat **49g** • Carbs **14g** • Dietary fiber **3g** • Sugars **5g** • Protein **73g**

Grilled Strawberries
with Smoked Whipped Cream

apple or another
fruitwood
WOOD PELLETS

**180°F (82°C);
450°F (232°C)**
GRILL TEMP

3 to 5 mins
COOK TIME

Grilling intensifies the sweetness of such fruit as strawberries and peaches. (See page 169 for **Grilled Peaches with Raspberry Sauce**.) And the smoked whipped cream? It's a revelation. However, you do need to make that ahead of time so the cream has ample time to chill.

Serves **4** • Prep time **10 mins** • Rest time **3 mins**

16 large strawberries, stems intact

aged balsamic vinegar or balsamic glaze

for the whipped cream
1 cup heavy whipping cream

1 tbsp powdered sugar, plus more

2 tsp orange-flavored liqueur (optional)

½ tsp pure vanilla extract

1. Preheat the grill to 180°F (82°C).

2. Place a baking dish on the grate and pour in the whipping cream. Smoke for 30 minutes, stirring once or twice. Transfer the cream to the bowl of a stand mixer and refrigerate until well chilled, about 1 to 2 hours.

3. Add the sugar, liqueur (if using), and vanilla extract. Whip the cream on medium-high to high speed until peaks form. (Don't overwhip.) Transfer the mixture to a serving bowl and refrigerate until ready to serve.

4. Preheat the grill to 450°F (232°C).

5. Wash and dry the strawberries. Thread 4 berries each on 4 bamboo skewers. Place the skewers on the grate and grill until grill marks appear, about 3 to 5 minutes, turning once or twice.

6. Remove the strawberries from the grill and drizzle with the balsamic vinegar. Serve with the smoked whipped cream.

TIPS | *Try to find large, unblemished strawberries with stems—the kind that are often dipped in chocolate. Don't wash the berries until you're ready to grill them. If you don't own an electric mixer, whip the cream with an old-school egg beater or a whisk.*

Nutrition per 4 strawberries
Calories **240** • Total fat **22g** • Carbs **10g** • Dietary fiber **2g** • Sugars **6g** • Protein **2g**

Bacon-Wrapped Onion Rings

I don't know who invented bacon-wrapped onion rings, which began making the rounds of barbecue chat rooms a few years ago, but they're owed a debt of gratitude. These onion rings are fantastic with burgers, steaks, or chops and they can be served on their own or as an appetizer.

hickory or maple
WOOD PELLETS

350°F (177°C)
GRILL TEMP

20 to 25 mins
COOK TIME

Serves **4** • Prep time **15 mins** • Rest time **none**

2 large sweet onions, peeled

3 tbsp unsalted butter

2 tbsp pure maple syrup

2 tbsp sriracha (optional)

1½lb (680g) thin-sliced bacon

1. Preheat the grill to 350°F (177°C).

2. Slice each onion crosswise into ½-inch-thick (1.5cm) slices. Carefully push the centers out of each slice, leaving the two outermost concentric layers. Reserve the 8 largest rings. Save the remainder for another use.

3. In a small saucepan on the stovetop over medium-low heat, melt the butter. Whisk in the maple syrup and sriracha (if using). Dip the onion rings in the butter mixture and let any excess drip off. Spiral each onion ring with bacon until the ring is covered. (You'll likely need more than one strip per ring.) Use a toothpick to secure the ends.

4. Place the onion rings on the grate and grill until the bacon is nicely browned and sizzling, about 20 to 25 minutes, turning once.

5. Transfer the onion rings to paper towels to drain and remove the toothpicks. Place the rings on a platter and serve.

TIPS | *An easy variation is buffalo-style onion rings. Using the method above, dip the onion rings in a one-to-one mixture of melted butter and your favorite hot sauce. Wrap in bacon and grill as directed. Serve with blue cheese dressing or dip and celery sticks.*

Nutrition per 2 onion rings

Calories **842** • Total fat **76g** • Carbs **16g** • Dietary fiber **2g** • Sugars **9g** • Protein **22g**

Rainbow Carrots
with Mustard Vinaigrette

There's a fine line between charred (good) and burnt (bad). Charring carrots really brings out their natural sweetness. Multicolored rainbow carrots are preferred for this recipe, but if they're not available, buy regular orange carrots. (They taste so much better than bagged carrots.)

apple or cherry
WOOD PELLETS

450°F (232°C)
GRILL TEMP

6 to 8 mins
COOK TIME

Serves **4** • Prep time **15 mins** • Rest time **none**

3 to 4 bunches of rainbow carrots (at least 20 total), scrubbed and tops trimmed

3 tbsp extra virgin olive oil

1 tbsp fresh thyme leaves

½ tsp coarse salt

½ tsp freshly ground black pepper

sprigs of fresh thyme

for the vinaigrette

2 tbsp balsamic vinegar

1 shallot, peeled and finely diced

1 garlic clove, peeled and finely minced

2 tsp coarsely ground whole grain mustard

1 tsp honey (optional)

½ cup extra virgin olive oil

coarse salt

freshly ground black pepper

1. Place a cast iron griddle or a large cast iron skillet on the grate. Preheat the grill to 450°F (232°C).

2. In a small bowl, make the vinaigrette by whisking together the balsamic vinegar, shallot, garlic, mustard, and honey (if using). Continue to whisk as you add the olive oil in a thin stream. Season with salt and pepper to taste. Set aside.

3. Place the carrots in a large resealable plastic bag. Add the olive oil, thyme, and salt and pepper, turning the bag several times to coat.

4. Place the carrots in a single layer on the griddle and grill until they're darkly browned on the bottom, about 4 to 5 minutes. (You don't want them to burn or they'll be bitter.) Turn and grill for 2 to 3 minutes more.

5. Transfer the carrots to a platter. Whisk the vinaigrette for a few seconds and drizzle over the carrots. Top with fresh thyme sprigs before serving.

TIPS | *You won't need all the vinaigrette. Refrigerate the remainder for up to 5 days. The vinaigrette is a great marinade for meat or poultry.*

Nutrition per 5 carrots
Calories **260** • Total fat **29g** • Carbs **2g** • Dietary fiber **0g** • Sugars **1g** • Protein **0g**

Brussels Sprouts & Bacon Skewers

oak, hickory, or pecan
WOOD PELLETS

400°F (204°C)
GRILL TEMP

8 to 10 mins
COOK TIME

When I was a child, there was always a jar of pickled Brussels sprouts in my Christmas stocking. But it was years before I began pairing them with bacon. This recipe also features a maple syrup butter. Entire stalks of Brussels sprouts can sometimes be found in supermarkets near the holidays. This way, you'll know they're fresh.

Serves **4** • Prep time **15 mins** • Rest time **none**

24 Brussels sprouts, about 1½lb (680g) total

1 to 2 tbsp extra virgin olive oil

coarse salt

freshly ground black pepper

6 strips of thin-sliced bacon

for the butter

4 tbsp unsalted butter

1 tbsp maple syrup or honey

½ tsp smoked paprika

¼ tsp ground cayenne, plus more

1. Preheat the grill to 400°F (204°C).

2. Trim the bottom off each sprout and remove any yellowed or blemished leaves. In a large saucepan on the stovetop over medium-high heat, bring enough salted water to cover the Brussels sprouts to a boil. Add the Brussels sprouts and parboil for 5 minutes. Drain well and let cool. Transfer the sprouts to a bowl. Toss with the olive oil. Season with salt and pepper.

3. Return the saucepan to the stovetop over low heat. Make the butter by melting the butter and stirring in the maple syrup, paprika, and cayenne. Keep warm.

4. Place the bacon strips on the grate and grill until partially cooked, about 10 minutes, turning once or twice. Transfer the bacon to paper towels to let cool. Cut into 1-inch (2.5cm) squares.

5. Alternate threading the Brussels sprouts and the bacon pieces on bamboo skewers. Place the skewers on the grate and grill until the Brussels sprouts are tender crisp and well browned and the bacon is fully cooked, about 8 to 10 minutes, turning as needed. Brush the skewers with the reserved maple butter the last 2 minutes of grilling.

6. Remove the skewers from the grill. Brush once more with maple butter before serving.

TIPS | *If you want to retain their bright green color, plunge the Brussels sprouts into ice water after parboiling and then drain again. While skewers look attractive, you can save time by placing the Brussels sprouts and bacon pieces into a grill basket. Grill until the Brussels sprouts are tender crisp and well browned and the bacon is fully cooked, about 8 to 10 minutes, stirring occasionally. Transfer to a bowl and pour the butter mixture over them. Stir gently to coat.*

Nutrition per 6 Brussels sprouts

Calories **332** • Total fat **27g** • Carbs **10g** • Dietary fiber **3g** • Sugars **5g** • Protein **13g**

Spaghetti Squash
with Alfredo Sauce

Fluffy strands of cooked spaghetti squash can stand in for pasta in many dishes—a godsend for people watching their carbs. Here, it's accompanied by a rich and cheesy alfredo sauce. Or toss the hot squash with butter and salt and pepper for an almost labor-free side dish.

hickory or oak
WOOD PELLETS

400°F (204°C)
GRILL TEMP

45 mins
COOK TIME

Serves **4** • Prep time **20 mins** • Rest time **none**

1 large spaghetti squash

1 tbsp extra virgin olive oil

coarse salt

freshly ground black pepper

1 tbsp chopped fresh curly or
flat-leaf parsley

¼ cup thinly shaved Parmesan
cheese

for the sauce

4 tbsp unsalted butter

2 garlic cloves, peeled and
minced

1 cup heavy whipping cream,
plus more

3oz (85g) light cream cheese,
cut into cubes

¾ cup grated Parmesan cheese

1 tsp dried Italian seasoning

pinch of freshly ground nutmeg

coarse salt

freshly ground black pepper

1. Preheat the grill to 400°F (204°C).

2. In a small saucepan on the stovetop over medium heat, make the alfredo sauce by melting the butter. Stir in the garlic and cook for 2 minutes. Stir in the whipping cream, cream cheese, Parmesan, Italian seasoning, and nutmeg. Season with salt and pepper to taste. Lower the heat to low and whisk until the sauce is smooth and the cheese has melted, about 6 to 8 minutes. If the sauce is too thick, add a bit more cream (or substitute milk). Keep warm.

3. Line a rimmed baking sheet with aluminum foil. Use a long-bladed chef's knife to slice the squash in half lengthwise. Scoop out the seeds from each half with a metal spoon. Brush the cut sides of the squash with olive oil and season with salt and pepper. Place the squash cut sides down on the baking sheet and pierce each half through the rind a few times with the tines of a fork to allow steam to escape.

4. Place the baking sheet on the grate and roast until the squash is tender when pierced with a fork, about 45 minutes.

5. Remove the sheet from the grill. Use a dinner fork to pull the spaghetti-like strands from the flesh of the squash. Transfer the strands to a shallow serving bowl. Use tongs to toss the squash with some of the alfredo sauce. Scatter the parsley and shaved Parmesan over the top. Serve immediately.

TIPS | *Like butternut or acorn squash, spaghetti squash is very dense and can be difficult to slice when raw. If desired, pierce the squash in several places with the tip of a knife. Microwave on high for 3 to 5 minutes. Let cool and then slice lengthwise. You might not need all the sauce. Cover and refrigerate any extra alfredo. Use it on other roasted vegetables, such as asparagus, cauliflower, fennel, or onions.*

Nutrition per ¼ squash and ⅓ cup sauce

Calories **523** • Total fat **50g** • Carbs **7g** • Dietary fiber **3g** • Sugars **0g** • Protein **11g**

Parmesan-Crusted Cauliflower

A whole head of cauliflower topped with a creamy cheese sauce and panko breadcrumbs makes an impressive side dish when served with grilled meats, such as chicken and pork. This dish can even step into the role of main course if you're looking for a meatless entrée.

oak
WOOD PELLETS

375°F (191°C)
GRILL TEMP

25 mins
COOK TIME

Serves **4** • Prep time **20 mins** • Rest time **none**

1 whole cauliflower, about 1½lb 680g)

3 tbsp unsalted butter, melted

1 tbsp freshly squeezed lemon juice

coarse salt

freshly ground black pepper

for the topping

3 tbsp unsalted butter, melted

¾ cup panko breadcrumbs

1 tsp garlic salt

¾ cup grated Parmesan cheese

¾ grated Monterey Jack or provolone cheese

½ cup ranch dressing

¼ cup minced fresh curly or flat-leaf parsley or chives

1. Preheat the grill to 375°F (191°C).

2. Remove any leaves from the base of the cauliflower and recut the stem so the cauliflower sits upright. In a large stockpot on the stovetop over medium-high heat, bring enough salted water to cover the cauliflower to a boil. Place the cauliflower in the water and use a pot lid to keep it submerged. Boil until the cauliflower is tender, about 12 minutes. (A bamboo skewer inserted in the cauliflower should meet little resistance.)

3. Transfer the cauliflower to a colander and drain stem side up until the outside is fairly dry. Place the cauliflower stem side down in a cast iron skillet. Combine the butter and lemon juice. Brush the outside of the cauliflower with the butter mixture and lightly season with salt and pepper.

4. In a small bowl, make the topping by combining the butter, breadcrumbs, and garlic salt. Stir to coat the breadcrumbs. Set aside.

5. In a small saucepan on the stovetop over low heat, combine the cheeses and ranch dressing. Stir the mixture until the cheeses are partially melted and the sauce has thickened, about 5 minutes.

6. Spread the cheese sauce over the cauliflower and sprinkle the panko mixture over the cheese. Place the skillet on the grate and roast the cauliflower until it's heated through and the cheese sauce and panko are lightly browned, about 25 minutes.

7. Remove the skillet from the grill and sprinkle the parsley over the cauliflower. Present the cauliflower whole and then slice it into wedges.

TIPS | *Substitute colored cauliflower—orange, purple, or green—for the white variety. Reduce the cooking times if the heads are substantially smaller. To get seasoning deep into the vegetable, treat it like a cut flower: Cut a thin slice from the stem and set it upright in heavily salted water for several hours or overnight. A wok works well for this. Drain and then proceed with the recipe.*

Nutrition per ⅙ cauliflower

Calories **576** • Total fat **47g** • Carbs **19g** • Dietary fiber **4g** • Sugars **6g** • Protein **20g**

Eggplant, Tomato & Mozzarella Stacks

Do you sometimes buy eggplant without a plan, seduced by how purple and voluptuous they look? You'll never be without a reason for purchasing eggplant again. These beautiful stacks of grilled eggplant, tomato slices, and fresh mozzarella will make sure of that.

oak
WOOD PELLETS

425°F (218°C)
GRILL TEMP

10 to 14 mins
COOK TIME

Serves **4** • Prep time **20 mins** • Rest time **none**

¼ cup extra virgin olive oil

1 large eggplant, trimmed and sliced into 8 rounds

2 large beefsteak tomatoes, sliced into 8 rounds

dried Italian seasoning

coarse salt

freshly ground black pepper

2 balls fresh mozzarella, each about 8oz (225gr), sliced into 8 rounds total

balsamic vinegar or balsamic glaze

fresh basil leaves

1. Preheat the grill to 425°F (218°C).

2. Pour the olive oil on a rimmed sheet pan and coat the bottom. Add the eggplant and tomato rounds and turn to thoroughly coat both sides. Lightly season on both sides with Italian seasoning and salt and pepper.

3. Place the eggplant and tomato slices on the grate and grill the eggplant until it has grill marks and has begun to soften, about 5 to 6 minutes per side. Grill the tomato slices for 3 to 4 minutes per side. (Work in batches if your grate is too small to hold all the vegetables at once.) Remove the vegetables from the grill and let cool. (Leave the grill going.)

4. Drizzle olive oil on a second rimmed sheet pan. Alternate the eggplant, tomato, and cheese to create 4 stacks with 6 layers each, ending each stack with cheese. Place the sheet pan on the grate and cook the stacks until the cheese softens and melts, about 5 to 8 minutes.

5. Transfer the stacks to plates. Drizzle with olive oil and balsamic vinegar. Scatter the basil over the top before serving.

TIPS | *Instead of fresh basil leaves, place a dollop of pesto (homemade if possible) on top of each stack.*

Nutrition per 1 stack
Calories **235** • Total fat **13g** • Carbs **16g** • Dietary fiber **6g** • Sugars **10g** • Protein **15g**

Grilled Peaches
with Raspberry Sauce

You don't have to forego dessert just because you're watching your carbs. This combination of fresh in-season peaches, jewel-like raspberries and raspberry sauce, and a dollop of mascarpone cheese will satisfy your craving for a post-prandial treat.

peach or
another fruit
WOOD PELLETS

450°F (232°C)
GRILL TEMP

6 to 8 mins
COOK TIME

Serves **4** • Prep time **10 mins** • Rest time **none**

4 freestone peaches

4 tbsp unsalted butter

¼ cup light brown sugar or low-carb substitute

½ tsp pure vanilla extract

pinch of coarse salt

4oz (110g) mascarpone cheese

sprigs of fresh mint

fresh raspberries

for the sauce

2½ cups fresh raspberries

3 tbsp distilled water

3 tbsp granulated sugar

1oz (30ml) raspberry liqueur

2 tsp freshly squeezed lemon juice

1. Preheat the grill to 450°F (232°C).

2. In a blender, make the raspberry sauce by combining the raspberries and water. Blend until the berries are puréed, using a spatula to scrape them down. Place a fine-mesh strainer over a bowl and pour the purée into the strainer. Press on the solids with the back of a spoon until no more liquid can be extracted. Discard the solids. Stir in the sugar, raspberry liqueur, and lemon juice. Cover and chill until ready to use.

3. Rinse the peaches and blot them dry with paper towels. Run a small knife from the stem of a peach, following the crease, around the pit. Separate the peach into two halves. Remove the pit and discard. Repeat with the remaining peaches.

4. In a small saucepan on the stovetop over medium heat, melt the butter. Stir in the brown sugar, vanilla, and salt. Cook the mixture until it resembles a glaze, about 2 to 3 minutes.

5. Brush the cut sides of the peaches with the glaze. Place them cut sides down on the grate and grill until they've developed grill marks, about 6 to 8 minutes. Use a thin-bladed metal spatula to remove them from the grill.

6. Place 2 peach halves in each of 4 dessert bowls. Stir a little of the raspberry sauce into the mascarpone and add the mixture to the bowl. Drizzle the remaining sauce over the top. Add mint and raspberries to each bowl before serving.

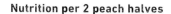

Nutrition per 2 peach halves

Calories **346** • Total fat **16g** • Carbs **45g** • Dietary fiber **7g** • Sugars **39g** • Protein **6g**

Grilled Fennel
with Grated Parmesan

apple
WOOD PELLETS

450°F (232°C)
GRILL TEMP

10 mins
COOK TIME

Fennel grows wild in the Mediterranean, where nearly all the plant is used, even its seeds (which give Italian sausage its distinctive flavor). My favorite way to prepare this vegetable loaded with vitamin C is to grill it until its tender and then dust it with a bit of freshly grated Parmesan.

Serves **4** • Prep time **10 mins** • Rest time **none**

3 large fennel bulbs

2 to 3 tbsp extra virgin olive oil

coarse salt

fresh coarsely ground black pepper

3oz (85g) finely grated Parmesan cheese

lemon wedges

1. Preheat the grill to 450°F (232°C).

2. Remove the outermost layer of the fennel bulb (it's usually quite fibrous). Trim the green stalks off the bulbs, reserving the feathery fronds. Cut a thin slice off the bottom of each bulb. Slice lengthwise through the core to cut the bulbs into ½-inch (1.25cm) slices.

3. Brush both sides of each fennel slice with olive oil and season with salt and pepper. Place the fennel on the grate at a slight angle to the bars. Grill until the fennel displays grill marks and begins to soften, about 4 to 5 minutes per side.

4. Remove the fennel from the grill and shingle on a platter. Sprinkle the Parmesan over the top. Place the reserved fennel fronds and lemon wedges around the edges. Serve warm or at room temperature.

TIPS | *Select larger fennel bulbs for this recipe. The stalks can be thinly sliced and used in stir-fries, soups, or salads. If desired, substitute orange wedges for the lemon wedges.*

Nutrition per 2 slices

Calories **167** • Total fat **12g** • Carbs **10g** • Dietary fiber **4g** • Sugars **0g** • Protein **8g**

Prosciutto-Wrapped Asparagus

oak
WOOD PELLETS

425°F (218°C)
GRILL TEMP

10 mins
COOK TIME

A platter of prosciutto-wrapped asparagus is so appealing, I've seen it eclipse the main course. For easy prep, buy medium-sized spears. Larger spears can work, of course, as can thinner spears. For the latter, I like to group them in threes so the meat-to-vegetable ratio still works.

Serves **4** • Prep time **10 mins** • Rest time **none**

¼ cup extra virgin olive oil, plus more

1 tbsp freshly squeezed lemon juice

¼ tsp coarse salt, plus more

24 stalks of fresh asparagus

12 thin slices of prosciutto, halved lengthwise

freshly ground black pepper

½ cup finely grated Parmesan cheese

fresh lemon zest, cut into long, thin strands

1. Preheat the grill to 425°F (218°C).

2. In a small bowl, whisk together the olive oil, lemon juice, and salt until the salt dissolves.

3. Trim the woody ends off the asparagus stalks. Place them in a single layer on a rimmed sheet pan. Pour the olive oil mixture over the asparagus and roll the stalks around to thoroughly coat. Spiral an overlapping half-slice of prosciutto around each asparagus spear, leaving the top and bottom exposed. (The prosciutto usually sticks to itself, so you shouldn't need toothpicks to secure it.)

4. Place the asparagus on the grate perpendicular to the bars and grill until the asparagus is bright green and tender crisp, about 10 minutes, turning as needed. (Cut the bottom off one spear to test its doneness.)

5. Transfer the asparagus to a platter. Lightly season with salt and pepper. Drizzle a little olive oil over the spears. Sprinkle the cheese and scatter the lemon zest over the top. Serve hot or at room temperature.

TIPS | *You can take this preparation in a Spanish direction by substituting orange juice and zest for the lemon, serrano ham for the prosciutto, and Manchego cheese for the Parmesan.*

Nutrition per 6 spears
Calories **161** • Total fat **10g** • Carbs **4g** • Dietary fiber **2g** • Sugars **2g** • Protein **15g**

Index

Acknowledgements

A huge debt of gratitude is owed to Steven Raichlen, my longtime mentor and friend, who taught me the joys of live-fire cooking and smoking and graciously penned the foreword to this book. Without him, I wouldn't have had the opportunity to write it.

I'm very grateful to the team at DK, an imprint of Penguin Random House, who had a vision for this book and saw it through: my patient and even-tempered editor, Christopher Stolle; talented art director William Thomas; and, of course, publisher Mike Sanders, who kept things on track.

Thanks also to compositor Ayanna Lacey, chef Alan Sternberg, food stylist Lovoni Walker, photographer Daniel Showalter, proofreaders Diane Durrett and Christopher Parris, and indexer Louisa Emmons.

Special thanks to Jason Baker of Green Mountain Grills, who provided pellet grills for recipe testing and for the photo shoot; to Mark Kelly of Lodge Manufacturing, who sent cast iron; to Robert Schueller of Melissa's Produce, who generously offered to supply beautiful fruits and vegetables; and to James Peisker of Porter Road Butcher, who bent over backward to get specialty cuts of meat to my door when I couldn't find them locally.

On the home front, my daughter, Samantha, and her partner, Kristin Calvert (who also took the author photo), were indefatigable food critics, eating pounds and pounds of protein during the recipe testing phase. Emotional support was provided from afar by my son, Matt, my dear mother, Shirley Nalley, and numerous friends, whose encouragement meant so much to me.

Finally, to my late husband, Lee Loseke, who always supported me unconditionally in everything I wanted to do. Sorry about all the grills on your side of the garage, hon.

About the Author

NANCY LOSEKE is a food journalist and recipe developer who owns more than a dozen grills and smokers—the majority of which are fueled by pellets. She was the research director of the James Beard Award–winning Rosengarten Report when she met author and barbecue expert Steven Raichlen in 2002. Since then, she has tested hundreds of recipes on a variety of equipment for his best-selling books, written a twice-weekly blog on barbecuebible.com, and is the culinary producer of his television shows, including *Project Fire*, *Project Smoke*, and *Primal Grill*. She jokes that she's an adjunct professor at Raichlen's popular Barbecue University, having assisted with the three-day "barbecue boot camp" more than two dozen times. Nancy is the former marketing director of pellet grill pioneer Traeger, where she laid the foundation for their extensive online recipe library and wrote the cookbook that accompanies all Traeger grills. She's a culinary school graduate and a recognized olive oil expert, with credentials from UC Davis. Nancy lives in Moreland Hills, Ohio, with her rescue cats and a dog.